"In *Death Did Us Part* Dr. Juma presents a case study of an African Christian couple living in Canada and facing the challenges of a broken relationship. They struggle with whether they can live together and wonder if the marriage has died. This struggle challenges their Christian faith and African family values. The book is a great read for therapists and for members of congregations who are called to walk with the couple through these difficult times. *Death Did Us Part* shows the complexities of the cultural clash between African Christian values and Western Canadian values around marriage and divorce. It does not provide any easy answers and yet shows the power of listening of a Christian caregiver."

—*Thomas St. James O'Connor, ThD, RP*
Professor Emeritus, Wilfrid Laurier University

DEATH
DID US PART

Deconstructing
the Mystery
Behind the Death
of a Marriage

FLORENCE A. JUMA, RP

DEATH DID US PART
Copyright © 2019 by Florence A. Juma, RP

All rights reserved. Neither this publication nor any part of this publication may be reproduced or transmitted in any form or by any means, electronic or mechanical, including photocopying, recording or any information storage and retrieval system, without permission in writing from the author.

Scripture taken from the New King James Version®. Copyright © 1982 by Thomas Nelson. Used by permission. All rights reserved.

Some names and identifying details have been changed to protect the privacy of individuals.

Printed in Canada

ISBN: 978-1-4866-1798-2

Word Alive Press
119 De Baets Street Winnipeg, MB R2J 3R9
www.wordalivepress.ca

Cataloguing in Publication information can be obtained from Library and Archives Canada.

To the memory of my mother,
Rosebella Awiti Owuor,
a paragon of beauty and strength.
She modelled the value of keeping vows, for better or worse.

CONTENTS

ACKNOWLEDGEMENTS ix
FOREWORD xi
INTRODUCTION xiii

CHAPTER ONE: AKAWD AND MUKA 1
CHAPTER TWO: A ROUGH START 9
CHAPTER THREE: ON LIFE SUPPORT 13
CHAPTER FOUR: THE FULL-CODE DIRECTIVE 21
CHAPTER FIVE: PHYSICAL ABUSE 27
CHAPTER SIX: EMOTIONAL AND PSYCHOLOGICAL ABUSE 33
CHAPTER SEVEN: FINANCES 39
CHAPTER EIGHT: SPIRITUAL RESILIENCE 45
CHAPTER NINE: THE FINAL BLOW 49
CHAPTER TEN: IN A COMA 59
CHAPTER ELEVEN: MY ANALYSIS 63

CONCLUSION 69
AFTERWORD 73
OTHER BOOKS BY THE AUTHOR 75

ACKNOWLEDGEMENTS

For the last ten years, I've had the honour of interacting with colleagues and associates who seek to commit themselves to the profession of helping couples and families experience healthy and thriving relationships. I'm grateful for the opportunity these interactions accord me. They have helped me achieve my ambition of becoming a lifelong learner in the helping profession. I owe my evolving perception to the many students in the field of pastoral care and counselling. Their insight and knowledge continually shape and broaden my perspectives on diverse and bourgeoning approaches to fostering health and wellbeing through couples and family therapy.

I'm eternally grateful to Word Alive Press for giving the manuscript that produced this piece a chance. Their team of editors and professionals turned my simple journal into something legible. They saw the potential in my work and trusted me with their resources.

―――― FOREWORD ――――

In my earlier memoir, *Away from Home: The Joys and Challenges of Migration*, I reflected on some of my family's experiences during our move from Africa to Canada. I also wrote about some of the joys and challenges that characterized our initial years of settlement in Canada.

Many of my fellow newer immigrants and colleagues from the African continent have echoed sentiments of similar experiences. Indeed, there are countless stories of opportunities as well as privations narrated among newer immigrants in their attempts to settle and rebuild their lives in a new environment.

Common among the narratives have been the challenges they face in couple and family relationships. Whereas some families have credited the success of their efforts to the ease with which they sought and identified relevant resources to help with their early settlement, many newer immigrants have encountered stiffer challenges. There are those who may feel stuck between the life that was and the life that is now evolving. Their well-intended attempts to integrate and successfully function within the worldview and perspectives of the two worlds seem to be challenged at every step. This phenomenon can make life difficult even for the most healthy, high-functioning couples and families, since developmental stressors tend to have a compounding effect when they're experienced in what may be considered a foreign context.

As with any new venture, the move to a new context presents an equal share of joys and challenges. The joys include new opportunities, meeting and making new friends, learning new skills, and sharing knowledge and resources. Challenges may include the lack of extended family or community support and the need to acquire new or relevant skills to enhance one's chances of thriving. For young families, additional resources may be required for effective entry, or re-entry, into the various programs and systems.

This book is a biography highlighting the marital experience of one couple. In it, I map the couple's journey through the challenges they encountered while living in Canada. The couple attempted to address these challenges through their culture's traditional approach, an approach that seemed to fall short of the expectations of the wife. Muka found herself overwhelmed with the path her husband chose.

The story demonstrates how well-intended methods of addressing relationship difficulties may fail. It also reveals how individuals cannot fully anticipate and prepare themselves for all life stressors. The couple in this story never anticipated a challenge that would threaten the life of their marriage. When it happened, every attempt to save their marriage failed.

It is interesting to note the prevalence of services and supports available to help couples facing these difficulties. However, at the time of this couple's greatest need, the support systems available to them seemed irrelevant. In the end, their marriage succumbed to the challenges and died.

The lessons learned from this experience have challenged me to think of alternative methods of providing therapy in a foreign context. The story may serve as a case study of potential pitfalls in the helping profession. It may further help by contributing to the tough conversations held by couples and therapists both at home and abroad.

INTRODUCTION

Marriage is considered a sacred institution, at least from within my Christian faith perspective, although it also exists within a legal and cultural framework. From a faith perspective, the marriage phenomenon is one that has been experienced and observed since the times of the first couple, Adam and Eve. In this book, I write from the standpoint of a contemporary evangelical Christian.

The following narrative is the personal account of a close friend, given with the hope that her story may serve as an example of the efforts taken by those who commit themselves to helping couples, professionals who endeavour to analyze the common factors that contribute to the breakdown of a marriage. I define marriage as the sacred union between two people who choose to live together and work out their relationship in a less than ideal, not so sacred world. As such, a married couple will encounter pitfalls along the way.

One of the oldest aspects of the marriage vow, each aspect of which is equally important, comprises these five words: "Till death do us part." This phrase expresses the desire of two people to remain committed to each other in marriage until one of them dies. Indeed, it is reasonable to believe that most people enter into marriage with the desire and hope of getting it right the first time and staying married until death. Countless couples have maintained their lifetime commitment to each other, some within their faith practice and others despite it. However, others have succumbed to the unexpected and sometimes unforeseen stressors that strain a relationship to the breaking point.

The statistics I've encountered present different narratives. In some, marriages are in a constant state of defence against challenges that deplete a couple's resources and supports. These are the stories that attracted my attention, leading me to make an extensive analysis, even a deconstruction, of these narratives. While pondering them, I encountered similar themes. I observed the similarity between physical death and marital death.

A physical death may take place when the heart stops beating or the lungs stop breathing. However, advancements in medical science have given us ways to keep these organs functioning with external support, thereby delaying or reversing the course of death. Of course, sometimes key organs fail despite the efforts and expertise of health professionals and the support of medical technologies.

In the same manner, therapists—those who devote their time and effort to upholding and sustaining healthy relationships—are required to foster hope, sometimes amidst challenging situations. Certain practices and lifestyles tend to foster relationship well-being.

In particular, love and forgiveness are helpful ingredients in healthy and long-lasting relationships. In most Christian traditions, a wedding ceremony presents an opportunity for a couple to emphasize their need for love and forgiveness in building a long and happy marriage. While love has the capacity to grow over a period of time, forgiveness is the prerogative of the individual choosing to offer it. The presence of love does not guarantee forgiveness. However, a loving environment is conducive to forgiveness.

Love is foundational in a trusting relationship. It precedes trust. Trust then serves as one of the key organs in the life of the relationship. A grounded trust can significantly enhance the ability of spouses to live through certain challenges. If love is the life-blood of the relationship, trust comprises the veins that carry it throughout the body. Should the trust in a relationship be broken, the relationship will suffer. There's even a chance that the love, proverbially speaking, will run out.

Similar to a physical body, it may be possible to resuscitate a relationship back to life. With good will and the presence of necessary supports, such an effort may yield positive results.

Some factors known to exert strain on relationships include internal and external stressors related to one's careers, in-laws, children, finances, friends, and hobbies. If these are not adequately addressed in the early stages of a relationship, they will compound with time. By the time any of these stressors threatens to destroy a relationship, it will most likely have developed resistance to therapeutic interventions.

This simple description of the causes and processes of death led me to an important question: is it possible for the life of a marriage to replicate physiological life, either thriving or dying despite the individuals? In other words, could a relationship be plagued with life-threatening maladies despite the love, good will, and intentions of the couple in that relationship? I mulled this over, thinking in particular of a dear couple whom I had known most of my adult life. Based on the experience of this couple, sadly, it seems that the answer to this knotty question is yes. It is a distressing and unfortunate answer indeed.

My dear friends Muka and Akawd seemed to share a deep love, the spiritual resilience of a thriving faith, and the good will of supportive family and an extended network of friends. They, like many young couples in love, believed that only physical death could ever come between them.

Hence, when Muka disclosed to me that Akawd had served her divorce papers and that their relationship was on the brink of the abyss, I was shocked. Muka seemed flustered. I had never seen her in such a state. She used the phrase "ambiguous grief" to describe the turmoil caused by the ordeal she was living through while awaiting the fate of her marriage.

The following pages present the account of Muka's narrative, recalling the factors that forced her and her husband's lives apart. I will approach this narrative from my unique blend of cultural and spiritual perspectives. Like Akawd and Muka, I too am an immigrant, originally from Africa, living my faith and practicing my profession in Canada. My personal journey in the Christian faith evolved from the Anglican tradition to the Pentecostal tradition during my adolescence years. I was credentialed by the Assemblies of God Church in Kenya and served in different pastoral roles for over a decade before moving to South Africa, where I completed a graduate degree in education and enrolled in a PhD program in historical theology. I then migrated to Canada where, like many immigrants, I found myself working menial jobs while completing my doctorate degree. My academic and professional journey led to my present positions of spiritual care practitioner in the healthcare system and associate professional faculty at a public seminary, where I teach part-time in the Department of Spiritual Care and Psychotherapy.

My motivation in attempting this case study is my own interest in exploring various therapeutic options, as I myself teach graduate courses on spiritual care and psychotherapy. This analysis will integrate African cultural approaches in psychotherapy with social sciences and African cultural norms transmitted through oral traditions. That said, the source of authority in my life is Christian theology as revealed and taught by the Bible, the Word of God.

CHAPTER ONE
AKAWD AND MUKA

Akawd and Muka migrated to Canada from Africa with their bourgeoning family at the dusk of the twentieth century. At the time of their migration, they had been married for nearly two decades and were each enrolled in a post-graduate program in theology. They completed their programs within three years of arriving in Canada and then made the decision to settle, temporarily, in Canada and raise their children. Their children have since grown into young adults, some married with young families.

Before coming to Ontario, Akawd and Muka had served their church in various capacities in their country of origin. In attempting to integrate into their new community, they sought out peers from a similar heritage. They served with a team of ministers that served the immigrant community. They faced many of the expected challenges in their migration and seemed to have handled them well.

Their professional journeys weren't as smooth. Like many immigrants, they went through the rigorous process of retraining to obtain relevant opportunities in their fields of practice. Whereas Muka succeeded in returning to her profession ten years after landing in Canada, Akawd's efforts didn't seem to yield the same results. As such, he redirected his focus toward other projects.

After nearly fourteen years in Canada, having raised and supported their children through their transitional years, the couple seemed prepared for the transition into the empty nest stage of their life. Their youngest child was attending school away from home and the other two were in the early stages of their careers, one completing an internship abroad, the other volunteering on another continent. All three children were independent enough to sustain themselves away from home.

It so happened that Akawd's employer began to restructure his company in preparation to relocate to another city. Some of its departments merged while others were phased out. Many employees were laid off, including Akawd. Muka proceeded to hold two jobs, working overtime to hold the fort. This replicated for them an earlier time; when they had first come to Canada, they had been in the same situation, as she had been the only one eligible for employment.

I met the couple around this time. Our respective families shared common experiences and Muka and I became close friends through the bimonthly women's fellowship we both attended. We lived in neighbouring cities and rode to the meetings together as often as we could. During one of these rides, Muka hinted that she and her husband were experiencing some challenges, although she believed that the situation was under control.

For the past two years, Akawd had been visibly absent from community events and functions. It had become common to see Muka by herself or with one or several of her children. Most people had stopped asking about Akawd. Even though Muka kept insisting that everything was under control, I had a feeling that something wasn't right.

Muka arrived late to the meeting one evening, bringing a store-bought fruit tray instead of her usual homemade snacks. This was a sign that there was a problem. I also noticed that Muka wasn't her usual jovial self that night; she seemed withdrawn and in low spirits. She slipped out just before the fellowship concluded.

I considered calling to check in with her, but then decided that it would be better to wait and call the following day. Knowing that her

CHAPTER ONE: AKAWD AND MUKA

Sundays were usually busy with church responsibilities, I waited until late in the evening to make the call. When we spoke, she confirmed that things were not as well as they should be, but she still felt that they were managing just fine. She didn't provide any details and I opted not to pry.

Several weeks later, I called on Muka and asked if Akawd had returned from a recent trip he had taken. It turned out that although he had come back, he wasn't home. He was in transition between jobs, so this wasn't uncommon. I just assumed he was on a job expedition.

Two weeks following this conversation, I decided it would be a good time to call and check with Muka again. I connected with her and asked if I could offer her a ride to the fellowship. To my surprise, she revealed that she had forgotten about it. This was so unlike her; she was always on top of her game.

"Is everything okay?" I asked, not able to believe that she could have forgotten something that was usually so important to her.

As much as I had sensed something was coming, nothing could have prepared me for the moment when she broke the terrible news.

"No, not really," she said. "He filed for divorce."

I was shocked and confused. Unsure if I had heard Muka right, I asked again, "Did you just say that Akawd filed for divorce?"

"Yes, I did. That is just one piece of the puzzle. He also entered bankruptcy protection, and he's handed his share of our property to the trustee in bankruptcy. It is a spiteful deed. It feels like he just pulled the rug out from under our feet without notice. I now co-own the house with a complete stranger who isn't interested in signing mortgage renewal papers."

To say I was shocked would be an understatement.

"He actually served me the papers a few months ago," she went on, surprising me even more. "When I first received the papers in the mail, I just ignored them, assuming it was a stunt. Luckily, he had filed them incorrectly and was required to do it again. I hoped that the matter would just go away. Oh how wrong I was. I learned the hard way that I should have responded more quickly. If a person doesn't respond within a month, it means that they legally agree to grant the divorce as requested. I discovered this just in time and managed to

3

respond before the deadline. I have hardly been able to process the significance of all this. And now I have to tackle this new bankruptcy challenge, too."

I was overcome with feelings of sadness, anger, and confusion. Even though we had communicated on the phone and by email, I hadn't seen Muka in weeks and was afraid to even imagine what she was going through. At the same time, I was at a loss for words. As much as I had suspected that things weren't good, I couldn't have imagined that the situation had deteriorated to the point of divorce.

I couldn't come up with anything meaningful to say, couldn't express the sympathy I felt inside. Instead I just listened as she reflected out loud, raising some crucial questions.

"How could this happen? How could my security have been so misplaced, my judgment been so wrong? I thought we had a relatively stable relationship, at least stable enough for each of us to remain committed to it. I should have taken him seriously when he threatened to do this. But how could I? His threats had stemmed from such ridiculous allegations. I had just assumed he would come to his senses and reconsider."

Oh how I wished that I could have come up with a sensible response. In desperation, I offered to visit her in person, which she welcomed. She didn't have any particular plans that day other than to stay home and reflect on her ordeal.

I decided to go to her house that cold Sunday afternoon and stay with her for the rest of the day. My purpose was merely to be present with her. I didn't have an agenda. I just wanted to offer some moral support, hoping that I could somehow console her as she processed the significance of the ordeal.

As I got ready to go, I felt anxious. What could I do to comfort her? What actions could I take to support her? My presence was truly all I could offer.

I was stunned and angry at Akawd for his unfathomable behaviour. What could possibly have gone wrong with him? Was he really so cruel? Did he perhaps suffer from some undiagnosed mental disorder? I wished in vain that there could be a reasonable explanation.

CHAPTER ONE: AKAWD AND MUKA

In keeping with our cherished custom of sharing African snacks during visits, I made porridge from millet flour and mandazis, a kind of African donut. This was the very snack Muka regularly brought to the women's fellowship. They'd always had a therapeutic effect on us. Preparing and sharing the food evoked fond memories of our lives back home and led to thought-provoking conversations.

While preparing and cooking the food, I had a nagging feeling that neither of us would have an appetite. I watched the raw pieces of white dough turn golden brown, still trying to figure out what I would say. I needed to speak words of deep compassion, to introduce a soothing breeze into a situation so engulfed in sadness.

The drive to Muka's house seemed much shorter than usual. It felt like my feet arrived at the door sooner than my mind did. Feeling confused and disoriented, I took a moment to gather myself before ringing the doorbell.

When Muka answered the door, she reached out to welcome me into her house with a hug. She led me to the kitchen, to the small oblong table where I put down the flask of porridge and the bowl filled with mandazis.

"I made enough of these for today—and for later, if needed," I said, breaking the silence. I then pointed to my handbag. "And I have some more mandazis in here."

"Thank you for bringing the snack," Muka whispered. "I've just made a fresh pot of ginger and lemon tea. The tea is hot and ready to be served. How about we have the tea now and the porridge later… would you like a cup?"

She invited me to sit down at the table and served two cups of the freshly made tea.

"How are you managing?" I asked tentatively, afraid to learn the answer.

She sighed deeply and was silent for an uncomfortably long moment. "I really thought the time apart would help him come to his senses. Instead things have deteriorated even further. How could I have underestimated his threats? How could I have been so wrong? How could he trash our relationship, without so much as a second thought?"

We sat in silence for another long minute.

She cleared her throat. "You know what would really help me right now?"

"Please tell me."

"If I could just talk through this situation with you," she said. "There's a lot you don't know, and a lot I'm still trying to figure out. Maybe it would help me better understand the situation. Would you have time for that?"

"Of course," I responded, nearly overcome with emotion myself.

I had known Akawd and Muka for more than a decade. Akawd was one of the few immigrant pastors offering spiritual leadership to our fellow immigrants. Newly arrived groups had been forming into local congregations, and by now the number of fellowships had mushroomed, spreading to different cities and taking on unique visions and identities. In time, Akawd had switched his focus from serving in those fellowships to concentrate on some development initiatives back in his home village.

In the last few years, our two families hadn't seen each other as much, occupied as we were with family and work. However, we had still made attempts to get together and stay in touch. We supported each other as much as we could.

Akawd and Muka had seemed settled as they approached their middle adult years. They were both well trained and had served in the church throughout their adult lives. While Akawd had seemed to be pulling away from public life, though, Muka had remained engaged and continued her volunteer work in their congregation.

As we shared tea in Muka's kitchen, my thoughts wandered to happier times. The scene seemed very familiar, since we'd sat at this table many times before to talk about life, pray, sing, play games, or just share meals. Today the mood was sombre and the house felt empty.

Muka had been like a mentor to me and she was my role model. I didn't feel confident enough to offer any support beyond listening. At least she felt comfortable doing this with me. After all, we shared faith, a heritage, and friendship.

"This kind of thing can shock even the most experienced marriage counsellor," she mused. "But Akawd shut down every suggestion I made about going for counselling. Given where we've ended up, I just need to reflect on everything out loud and see if it makes sense to you, as an objective bystander. Your offer to listen is a big help. Thank you."

"No, Muka, I thank you for the privilege of being here with you."

With these words, it seemed like Muka was ready to begin her story—to deconstruct this mystery and figure out which of their many challenges had succeeded in dealing the fatal blow. It had to have been a sinister blow, since I had felt that their relationship had more positive aspects than negative ones. My initial hypothesis was that their relationship had cracked under the pressure of multiple stressors.

Now I just needed to get the whole story.

CHAPTER TWO
A Rough Start

Muka stared into her cup for a few minutes before taking a sip. She then set the cup on the table gently, keeping her hands wrapped around it. She seemed to be lost in thought.

I took a sip from my cup and broke the silence by expressing appreciation for the unique blend of ginger and lemon in the tea.

"This tea is special," I acknowledged.

"Yes, it is," Muka replied. "It's from the batch I brought back during our last trip."

We exchanged a glance as her eyes moved towards the living area and rested on Akawd's portrait on the wall.

She took a deep breath, as if to muster some courage. It seemed as though she was checking with herself, giving herself permission to start.

"It's tough to take stock of such a long relationship after more than thirty years of marriage," she began rather thoughtfully. "I think I'll begin with the year before our wedding."

"Sounds like a good place to start," I affirmed.

"Ours was a humble wedding, held in the pastor's office on a Friday afternoon. The wedding was witnessed by the spouse of the Dean of Students from the college we both attended and a member of the Board of Deacons at our church. The intimate ceremony included two other members of the board and the sitting missionary. My mother walked me into the office, holding my hand closely. Two of my Junior Choir members followed behind me as my bridesmaids." Muka sighed and adjusted her seat forward. "It's the silliest thing, but on our wedding day the weather kept alternating between clouds and sun—like nature itself couldn't make up its mind. Ever since that day, I have envisioned that as a kind of metaphor for our relationship."

She paused and looked down for a few minutes, as if to allow that piece of information to sink in. She then raised her eyes, offering a faint smile.

"Ironically, the weather outside reflected what I felt inside—overcast with periods of sun and clouds. Hmm. I entered one of the most sacred, legally binding, and culturally crucial relationships of my life with mixed feelings. Mixed feelings have been a constant theme running through our marriage. Looking back, I can see now that ineffective communication was one of our many recurring challenges. It plagued us right from the start. Our communication was poor, and at times it seemed to break down altogether. I often felt defeated when my efforts to express myself were either opposed or shut down. The alternative approach, of taking a firm stand, came at a high emotional cost.

"Our very first major disagreement is a good example of how ineffective our communication patterns were. It stemmed from an incident that occurred about a year before we got married. We couldn't even agree on the wedding date. I know, this must sound silly. I didn't take it seriously at the time, either, although I later learned just how significant it was for Akawd. He drew conclusions from that silly disagreement.

"To use a medical analogy, I would say our marriage was on life support from the beginning. We were ill-equipped to realize it at the time, though. We didn't have any premarital counselling, but neither did any of our peers. We were a generation in transition, from the earlier period when the extended family provided such supports to our modern times when pastors were trained in the skills of pastoral counselling. Indeed, Akawd and I were the first in our circle to take courses in counselling. It was assumed that we had all the knowledge and skills we needed. Our pastors believed we were more knowledgeable in interpersonal relationships than they were! That may have been true, but we only used our training for the benefit of others, not ourselves. We didn't yet have the option of seeking professional help for ourselves, and it turns out we were in dire need of professional help."

I sat back and listened as she narrated the story and helped fill in some of the gaps, describing the period around their wedding.

"Our wedding itself was less than ideal," she said. "I preferred to wait longer before getting married, and Akawd preferred an earlier date. He reasoned that my disagreement with him proved that I was strong-willed. He thought that he needed to break my will and conform me into his perception of an 'ideal wife'—a submissive wife. But he only admitted all this after the wedding, which in itself seemed a little sinister to me. I was hurt that he would intentionally do something like that.

"You see, the year before the wedding, Akawd had suggested an immediate wedding date, but I convinced him to wait just a little longer," she said. "I had some personal goals that I wanted to achieve before beginning our married life. I was in college, enrolled in a program that I hoped to complete in just one year. This would help me to gain some financial traction and allow me to financially support my parents, who were transitioning into retirement. I envisioned that Akawd and I would have a reasonable degree of financial stability and helpful independence from our families. But I had only a meagre income while I was still in college. I was twenty years old and believed we had ample time to plan a wedding and settle down.

"Well, I thought at the time that Akawd understood this. In fact, he was envisioning an opposite scenario. He really wanted to get married right away. He believed that we could do a better job planning, and providing for our extended family, once we were married. He, too, had some financial responsibilities from his family, and he was also a student, but he reasoned that we could work towards financial stability as a couple and share our responsibilities.

"My responsibilities were greater than his. As you know, in our culture older siblings are expected to assume financial responsibility for their younger siblings, providing aging parents with a bit of respite. Well, I came from a larger family than Akawd, and at the time of our marriage a good number of my siblings were still dependents. In fact, the youngest was just beginning elementary school.

"Like most of our peers in our culture, I accepted all this. It was to be a challenge for us to resolve, something we would have to learn to live with in the relationship—a relationship, we had come to see, that wasn't necessarily perfect. But we owned it and worked on it. I accepted that being in a relationship meant taking the good with the bad.

"When Akawd made his admission to me, though, he did it during an argument. Because of that, I wasn't sure if it was just careless talk or if he really had schemed and then acted on a plan he'd devised. Love and forgiveness would have come in handy, but I must admit that this whole incident put a dent in my trust in him. It felt like a betrayal."

I nodded, taking this all in. "I'm really sorry that you had to live with that experience. I hope you had opportunities to work through it."

"Well, we didn't necessarily have the most effective communications patterns, as I said. But I believed that we did process this and work through it."

Muka's narrative confirmed my initial perspective that marriage could take on a life of its own, either thriving or diminishing despite the efforts of the couple.

The cups were nearly empty by this time and the remaining tea cold. I moved mine to the side and brought my chair closer to the table, reaching to place my hand in hers. I wanted to affirm that I was in tune with her.

"You used the phrase 'on life support,' is that right?"

She nodded again and rose from her seat to refill the cups with hot tea. I drifted in my thoughts temporarily, coming back to the present as she served the tea again. I was thinking about their wedding, the day when two individuals had committed themselves to each other without knowing that their relationship was already in need of support.

As Muka refilled the cups, she sat down again and picked up where she had left off.

CHAPTER THREE
ON LIFE SUPPORT

We continued the narrative, with Muka poignantly discussing the process by which their relationship fell victim to their limited insight in effective communication. She admitted that her own approach in addressing their early challenges hadn't been ideal.

"After the wedding, I came up with a solution that I believed would help me avoid the emotional stress of disagreeing with Akawd. I decided to just maintain the peace by conceding. It was a pathetic solution, but I believed it was for the greater good. You see, this strategy seemed to be consistent with our culture's patriarchal traditions, where a family's life rotated around the men; women had to learn to find their step within the relationship without disturbing that rhythm.

"Know that I considered myself a feminist from a very young age, a biblically sound feminist, and I acknowledged and respected balanced principles when it came to gender roles. I never imagined myself living the stereotypical patriarchal practices that had informed our grandparents' and parents' lives. As such, I tried using my voice to stand up for myself. I tried letting Akawd know that I expected better for myself and my children. He called this rubbish, on the basis of his superior education. He believed that his better education relegated me and my recommendations to a junior place in the relationship. I therefore settled and took a passive approach.

"That strategy seemed to work, to a certain extent. It also explains why we're back in this place, faced with yet another life-altering decision. My beloved Akawd, the same one who coerced me into a hasty wedding and later admitted he'd done it to break my will, is now walking out on our relationship after more than three decades of marriage. Throughout our relationship, Akawd has found a way to get whatever it is he wishes for. In that same manner, he has now devised a plan to end our relationship and play the victim at the same time. You see, he's come up with what must have seemed like a foolproof scheme. He's made wild allegations against me that I never thought anyone could believe, and he has shared them widely, with anyone who cared enough to listen, convincing quite a few in the process. He's using it to blame me for the separation."

Muka stopped for a few minutes and looked down into her cup of tea, which had once again cooled. She hadn't taken a single sip from the fresh cup. She rose up from her chair to place the cup on the kitchen counter.

I followed her every move with my eyes, waiting to hear more about this so-called foolproof scheme.

She sat back down and continued narrating. "I didn't take him seriously at first, so I just ignored the allegations. But then Akawd began to act on them."

How could this happen? I wondered to myself. *How could she not even have suspected that he would act on the allegations?*

I held my thoughts, keeping them to myself until I got the full story.

"I didn't suspect that Akawd would do this," she continued. "If anything, I sympathized with him. I thought it would be really sad if he actually believed the allegations he was spreading about me—sad that he would try to leave the marriage in the same way he'd entered it, with a scheme.

"To his credit, Akawd had hoped to get married right away, start a family, and then continue supporting his family. This was a good aspiration that, unfortunately, didn't align well with what I had envisioned. It didn't help that I was five years younger than him and had put myself through high school, at least informally…"

That last statement seemed to trigger something in Muka, who rose from her seat and walked towards the living area. She stopped by the wall where their family picture hung. She placed her hand on the picture, resting it on Akawd's face.

"I get it," she continued. "He came from a polygamous family and his priority was to disengage himself from what may not have been an ideal family situation and start a dream family of his own. I, on the other hand, had grown up in a very supportive and loving family. I wanted to provide my parents with some financial comfort. Also, after putting myself through informal school I wanted to make sure my younger siblings all had the support they needed to obtain a formal education. If Akawd and I could wait a couple of years, I could do this."

Muka excused herself to freshen up. While she was gone, I retreated back into my thoughts. I gave some more consideration to the practice of supporting one's family, as Muka had described. In differently structured societies like the one she and I came from, family members helped meet the needs of their extended family. It was never meant to be an obligation, and it wasn't expected of someone if it was beyond their means. The system was based on honour, respect, and generosity. Siblings would help each other improve their lives. Through efficient communication, trust, and good will, familial responsibilities were shared based on each person's individual abilities and resources.

Children were deemed to be dependent on their parents until they had completed high school, for those who made it that far, or until their formal education came to an end. Muka's formal education had been terminated early in high school and she had been forced to work odd jobs during her mid-teens. Akawd, on the other hand, had completed higher education and acquired technical training. He, too, had worked for some time and contributed to the needs of his family.

Muka returned to the kitchen and sat in her chair. She placed her right elbow on the arm of the chair and raised her forearm, forming a fist. She then rested her cheek against the fist.

"Our different perspectives created tension," she continued in a defeated voice. "I didn't believe this tension would ever threaten our love for each other, though. I really believed it was just a minor bump on the road to what would be a healthy and happy relationship. As my father often said, it was important to learn how to resolve disagreements and reach resolutions early, when we had the time and luxury to do so. And I thought that learning how to negotiate conflicts would be a helpful skill.

"That is, until Akawd admitted that he had schemed to change my mind. I remember feeling a wave of disappointment when he disclosed this. He had thought that breaking my will would ensure a better relationship in the long run. Well, how well did that work out, given that we're now at the brink of divorce?

"I also wonder if I should have followed the wisdom of our oral traditions more closely. Would that have made a difference? If so, what kind of a difference would it have made? I really do wonder how it all went wrong. I just don't understand how the relationship derailed. We should be celebrating our thirty-fourth wedding anniversary right now, but instead here I am, reminiscing about old times.

"I hope you understand how committed I've been to the success of our marriage. Despite the hiccup at the onset of our life together, our love for each other had been solid and robust. However, with the strained trust between us, we haven't been able to fight for our marriage very well."

I wanted to understand how Muka could still believe in their love, after all that had happened.

"Muka, would you mind telling me more about the resilience of your love, and the resources that were in place for you and Akawd in the early years of your relationship?" I asked.

She nodded. She wanted to talk about this more clearly to understand it herself and nail down the causes of her marital breakdown.

"You see, even though my trust in him was dented, I still believed there was enough good will between us. We had all the time in the world, and so much youthful energy, to work on our relationship. Our love hadn't run out. It had the potential to survive. Our trust wasn't completely broken. After all, we had taken a vow to love each other for

CHAPTER THREE: ON LIFE SUPPORT

better or worse, till death do us part. We had come into the relationship with a full-code directive."

That phrase—full-code directive—caught my attention. I thought it was interesting that she should use the phrase, because it was strangely familiar to me.

"What do you mean by 'full-code directive'?" I asked. "Does that mean a zero tolerance for separation or divorce?"

Muka gave me a faint smile of affirmation, then recommended that we move into the living room and make ourselves more comfortable. We both realized this was going to take longer than we had thought.

I followed her to the couch, where we settled down comfortably.

"By full-code directive, I meant that our relationship was to be resuscitated at all costs," she said. "Our cultural values and faith practices reinforce this stance. Our oral traditions don't magnify the roses over the thorns, after all."

We had both heard the analogy comparing marriages to rose bushes.

"One thing I took for granted, although it turned out to be helpful, was lowering my expectations in order to guard against disappointment," she said. "This was conveyed to me three times by different people in my extended support network.

"I had many conversations with Mr. C, a cook in my college cafeteria, before Akawd and I were married. Mr. C would, in a casual and light-spirited manner, tell me that Akawd may not be as charming once he was my husband. He said this with such authority! He was just trying to help, taking the role of an elder in my life. I should have taken him seriously, especially because he belonged to the same cultural heritage as Akawd. He had a valuable perspective. In that culture, Mr. C explained, a woman's opinion didn't count in a marriage. Total submission wasn't only expected, it was required. I see now that he was only trying to help lower my expectations, to avoid shock later on. At the time, I just laughed it off, telling him that I thought he was wrong. I thought that there had been too much generational change, change brought about through social sciences and the influence of Scripture, for those old views to still be true. Mr. C, however, insisted that he was a good judge of character, and he felt that Akawd would opt to live by more rigid gender roles. 'I

17

can teach you some of the ways of our people,' he offered, 'including customs around home management, communication, child-rearing, etcetera.' He said this in a humorous, even exaggerated manner, but he remained persistent about it. According to him, I shouldn't expect Akawd to listen to and respect my opinion once we were married.

"I wasn't naïve when it came to dysfunctional relationships. I had witnessed quite a few dysfunctional relationships in the community. But I had been raised in a sheltered environment governed by strong Christian principles and positive cultural norms. Therefore, I reasoned that Mr. C didn't have a good point of reference. Perhaps his personal experiences had been negative. But it turned out that the patterns of my marriage did conform to Mr. C's predictions.

"Another conversation I had was with my mother-in-law, Mama G, after the birth of our second baby. We had made a trip to Akawd's parents' village. It was a joyous occasion, given that we were now the parents of two children, a toddler and an infant. While giving us advice about relationships and parenting, I specifically remember Mama G holding my hand and saying, 'My son is bad-tempered and quarrelsome. Protect yourself and the children from him.' I just laughed it off, finding this to be somewhat ridiculous. Mama G actually suggested that I try not to be in the same room with Akawd when he showed signs of anger. According to her, I was to gather the children and move to another room, locking the door behind us.

"In all fairness, I did respect Mama G's advice, but I believed that I had a more effective approach when it came to conflict resolution. I believed that the two of us had the advantage of having undertaken training in pastoral counselling and interpersonal relationships. I believed that we could utilize the knowledge and skills learned from these training programs and apply them to our own relationship.

"I thought that Mama G's advice was a product of another time, something that had worked well in her generation. You see, our parents had done an exceptional job at providing for us, at making our lives better through modern education. As such, Akawd and I were expected to be better informed when it came to modern practices and faith principles. Fortunately, though, most of the adults in our lives didn't have full

CHAPTER THREE: ON LIFE SUPPORT

confidence in our modern education, so they took every opportunity to give us counsel and advice. It didn't matter whether we'd asked for it. They just offered all the wisdom they could.

"The last and most surprising conversation I had was with a member of the congregation we served at the time. Mrs. L was the leader of the church's women's programs and a successful entrepreneur. During a conversation at the end of a women's meeting, Mrs. L made a casual comment about relationships: 'Don't you ever consider your husband a true friend, because men are not friends. They will extract all the good in you and abandon you the minute they feel your value has dropped.' I was appalled. I thought this judgment of men was rather harsh, if not outright cruel. I didn't make a comment. I was too surprised to believe that someone would think so lowly of another human being.

"The older generation she was from had shared a different way of life. For starters, most of them had followed the path of arranged marriages and had very little, if any, appreciation for so-called love marriages. Don't get me wrong: I held their counsel in good faith and considered myself fortunate to have had the opportunity to be nurtured by those who had experienced relationships from a different perspective. I also believed that this perspective would reinforce my appreciation for what Akawd and I shared and serve as a reminder of how far we had come. In fact, I felt that we were ready for any surprises that marital life might unveil.

"So, to answer your question, yes, I believed that we had many supports in place and that our love had the resilience to survive. Given our unique cultural heritages and shared faith, our relationship had a good chance of survival, safeguarded by the examples of other marriage before ours. Unfortunately, being aware of these cultural factors wasn't enough to prevent them from straining our own relationship.

"Akawd got his wish for a fast wedding, but it created a rift between us. He had learned that he could get his way by imposing his wishes on me or resorting to tantrums. I, on the other hand, had resorted to concealing my feelings. I didn't feel that he had considered my point of view or given me a choice. I discovered that my opinions and perspectives were to be shelved for the greater good. It soon became a relationship in which I felt silenced, and I often wondered if Akawd ever made an attempt to understand my feelings or positions.

"Moving forward, we struggled to negotiate our roles in the relationship, and this went on against the backdrop of our growing family. Welcoming our children into our lives were among the most memorable and defining moments in our relationship, and there was no doubt about our commitment to this young family. We dedicated ourselves to doing right by our children. Yes, we loved them dearly and attempted to raise and provide for them as best we could."

Muka tightened her grip on the sofa cushion as she talked about her children, as though overwhelmed by emotion. She paused for a few moments to regroup, reaching for the box of tissue that sat on the coffee table. She wiped away the tears that had begun to flow down her cheek.

"Is this becoming too much?" I asked. "Do we need to stop?"

"No," she assured me. "If anything, I need to keep going, while the memories feel fresh and relevant."

It was well past dinnertime by now, so I offered to serve some of the comfort food I'd brought. Muka welcomed the suggestion and we walked back toward the kitchen.

As she cleaned the kitchen table and replaced the tablecloth, I reached out and gave her a hug. I also wanted to assure her that everything was going to be okay. But I just couldn't.

"I'm really sorry," I whispered instead. "I wish you didn't have to go through all this."

She smiled and whispered back, "Thanks. I'm glad you're here."

CHAPTER FOUR
THE FULL-CODE DIRECTIVE

After handing her a cup of porridge, we made our way back to the living room and took our seats on the couch.

She took a sip of the porridge and I gave her the space to enjoy the drink before it cooled down again. I occupied myself with a family album I found in the cabinet underneath the coffee table. I wanted to pay attention to the picture, but instead my mind kept returning to the concept of the full-code directive. Her belief that divorce wasn't possible had given Muka a false sense of security. She had believed that her marriage was secure and based on her and Akawd's love for each other and their children, undergirded by their faith in God and belief in the Scripture, not to mention their roles as church leaders and their respect for their traditional practices and values. Surely even if they were to disregard one or two of these supports, there would remain several others.

"Tell me more about this full-code directive," I said upon noticing that Muka wasn't drinking the porridge anymore. "Did you think there was a point in your marriage when would you might forego it?"

She had taken a few sips and now fiddled with the half-empty cup.

"Even though our relationship began on life support, there was enough good will between us to revive it back to good health," she said.

"I loved Akawd and was willing to forgive him and start rebuilding trust again. Believing that love and forgiveness were an important remedy in marriage, I convinced myself that our relationship had a good fighting chance. Besides, our cultural values and religious beliefs guaranteed the survival of our marriage.

"Most importantly, we shared a deep love for each other and for our family. It seemed like only death could bring about the end of our marriage—at least, that's what I believed. Don't get me wrong: I was aware of the challenges of interpersonal relationships and the need to continually work on improving what we shared. However, Akawd continually reminded me that he couldn't imagine a life without me. He couldn't imagine being left a widower. He admitted that if it were up to him, he would prefer to die than go on without me. He was very convincing."

At this point, Muka gently turned towards me and asked, "Do I come across as a naïve person? Is it possible he was lying this whole time? If he was, how could I have missed it?"

I assumed these to be rhetorical questions and didn't attempt to answer them. Instead I placed my hand on Muka's shoulder to reassure her of my empathy and belief in her judgment.

We sat in silence for a few minutes, although it felt like a full hour.

"Did you believe that you both had the necessary skills and resources to sustain the marriage in the event of major challenges or life stressors?" I asked, softly rubbing her upper back.

Muka responded with a deep sigh. She seemed to search her inner being, almost as if she were scanning the many years of her marriage. Then she began by reflecting my questions back to me.

"I wonder," she said. "We never really thought that through. We just took it for granted. If anyone would have asked us if our relationship could survive such challenges, or if we had the resources to weather the marital storms, we would have responded in the affirmative. We weren't thinking ahead. We didn't consider the possibility that our marriage could succumb to a life stressor.

"And yes, I thought we did have all the resources we needed, that we were equipped for the journey ahead. We had spiritual and cultural

CHAPTER FOUR: THE FULL-CODE DIRECTIVE

resources, a faith connection and community, family support, and a social network. And most of all, we loved each other. Akawd and I were equipped with scriptural principles undergirding our religious understandings and beliefs. We had taken relevant courses in pastoral care and counselling, interpersonal relationships, effective communication, and conflict resolution—at first at the undergraduate level, then later at the graduate level. We also had the good will of our supportive extended family and friends. Our spiritual beliefs and faith practices provided us with positive, healthy, God-honouring life skills that sought to both build up our lives individually as well as the lives of our families and communities.

"Both Akawd and I were professing Christians when we met in our youth. Since we attended the same faith community, I assumed we were both grounded in the same scriptural teachings and were starting our life together on a solid foundation. With that understanding, I believed that our first line of defence would be the Scriptures, with our knowledge in counselling as a backup."

She reached for the Bible inside the cabinet beneath the coffee table. She continued, holding the book by her side.

"I know it now sounds like empty hope, but I believed in the teachings of this book," she said. "Scripture stipulates relationships of mutual love and respect between spouses, parents, children, and families. Furthermore, Scripture models selfless love and submission between spouses, which should yield a healthy and stable environment for a family. It further affirms that spouses should thrive as individuals and as couples. I really believed that we were on the same page in our understanding of these scriptural principles.

"My hope for a happy and healthy relationship was based on my belief that Scripture should be the first and last line of defence. It seemed to me that if the Scriptures weren't able to provide a sufficient remedy, other resources, however well-meaning they may be, would be highly unlikely to succeed. Florence, we weren't just members of the church, we were *leaders*. We were entrusted to guide people. If we couldn't make it in our marriage, how could we be entrusted to help others succeed? We were expected to lead by example."

Muka rose from her seat and walked across the room toward the window. She leaned on the window frame, allowing sunlight from outside to light her face and illuminate her teary eyes.

"Am I making sense? Does any of this make sense to you or does it just sound like I'm rationalizing?"

"No, it doesn't sound like rationalizing to me," I assured her. "If anything, you're helping me to understand my own worldview better, to clarify my perspective on marriage. After all, I share the same beliefs you do."

"I know," Muka said calmly. "That's why it's easier to talk about this with you. I don't have to explain everything. Believe me, I entered marriage fully aware that it would take more than our love and a support network to get through life. You see, the philosophy of a full-code directive is supposed to serve as a safety net. It doesn't assume the absence of challenges; rather, it anticipates challenges and seeks to equip couples with the skills and resources they need to fight back. It was on the basis of this understanding that I believed our marriage to be divorce-proof. I thought he and I shared this perspective. Brimming with love and forgiveness, I felt so secure about the relationship.

"Until now. Our marriage has now suffered a devastating blow, one so severe that it's destabilized every stronghold and support system I believed we had in place." She paused, taking a deep breath. "Here's a bit of irony. On a wall in my church, there's a framed placard containing a statement about the sanctity of marriage and the commitment of couples to remain together. The placard bears the signatures of many couples, including mine and Akawd's. I took a picture of it with my phone few weeks ago to remind myself of what we stood for."

While listening to this candid and exhaustive review of her marital challenges, I wondered if, in the process of withstanding so many onslaughts, the immune system of their relationship had just about reached its capacity. Muka had believed that their seasons of challenges had made their marriage stronger, but now she had to reflect back on them and wonder if she'd been wrong in her assessments. Had she missed the mark?

At least she was stopping now to take stock. This exercise was turning out to be helpful for both of us. I felt honoured that she'd invited me to join her in this journey.

But her story was disheartening, to say the least. I tried my best to remain composed and withhold reactions and judgments.

CHAPTER FIVE
PHYSICAL ABUSE

In addition to being rooted in a cultural heritage with zero tolerance for divorce, Akawd and Muka had been immersed in a faith tradition that disapproved of infidelity and encouraged supportive, life-enhancing family relationships. They also had a self-healing system in their culture, one that was intended to anticipate and address problems before they happened through the use of preventive therapeutic methods. Various individuals in the extended family had been designated with the responsibility to help address interpersonal conflicts.

The question therefore baffled me: did these two merely fall through the cracks of the self-healing system?

"There were instances during our relationship when I really believed that we needed the help of a professional therapist or marriage counsellor," she said. "The closest we came to accessing help was a conversation with our pastor during our early days in Canada. It didn't go well because Akawd felt like the pastor didn't see things from his perspective. He concluded that the pastor was biased. We didn't make any headway and the effort seemed futile."

She paused for a moment, as if to process the information she was about to share.

"You don't have to tell me any of this," I said.

"I know, and thank you for caring," she reiterated. "But I'd like to, if you're okay with it. There are just so many questions on my mind. I must admit that I'm reluctant to divulge this next part of the story, because a relationship is a sacred union between two people. Akawd and I deserve the privilege of keeping certain personal information between us, and it may not be fair that he isn't here to give his account of the narrative. If I was to hold this information inside, though, and wait for a time when Akawd is ready, it may never happen!"

Muka paused for a short while to gather herself.

"I wonder what would have happened if we'd just let the relationship end in its early years," she mused. "To be honest, the first ailment that plagued our relationship was physical abuse. This is my perspective, and Akawd may describe it differently. I understand that this isn't a therapy session and I'm not expecting you to take a side or feel the need to give advice. Bear in mind that this is just my perspective, as a victim. Akawd has told his side of the story to many of our family and friends. These are the 'allegations' I mentioned earlier. Out of respect and to avoid scandal, I kept those allegations to myself, believing they were too outrageous for anyone to believe. I had hoped that if people wanted to verify their accuracy, they would come to me; to my surprise, quite a few of his immediate family and ministry colleagues believed him, and their belief has given him the boldness to act.

"Although we came from different upbringings, we shared similar faith convictions. But in difficult times, it seemed as though Akawd reverted back to what he believed had worked effectively for him in his early life, a period when he had learned that responding to people in a physical way was an effective defence mechanism. I learned this the hard way very early in our life together, when we were expecting our first child. One evening, an argument ensued and Akawd reacted by slapping me in the face. When I attempted to call him out, he placed his hand over my lips, either in a panic or in an attempt to keep me from making a scene. Shortly after that, he apologized profusely and admitted that he had been wrong. He begged for forgiveness and promised it would never happen again. He then professed his love and commitment to me, our marriage, and our soon-to-be family. As it turned out, this was just the first of several physical assaults, and they were always followed with apologies and professions of love.

"The worst incident, the one that became seared in my mind, happened on a weekend when Akawd's younger brother was visiting. In a moment of heated argument, Akawd hit me in the presence of his brother. His brother intervened, standing between us, and attempted to reason with Akawd, but Akawd yelled back at his brother in his mother tongue, stating something to the effect of, 'Shut up, little brother. You know that women get beaten all the time.' I didn't have a good command of the language, but I did understand what my husband said that day. And it meant that the physical assaults would continue. It was going to be a way of life, and he would likely repeat this behaviour moving forward to express frustration with me or to get his way. I wept myself to sleep that night.

"At the time, we already had two precious children under our care. I cried both for myself and for them. I loved my children and tried as much as I could to keep them from witnessing any abuse. When I awoke early the next morning, I decided to take the children to my parents' house for a visit. Deep down, I was hoping to go home and return to a time before all these heartaches had happened. I wanted to relive, even if just for one day, the time I'd spent in my father's house, where I had felt safe and at peace. I wanted the children to spend some time in an environment that was as happy as could be. I wanted them to listen to my siblings make silly jokes and laugh.

"It had been a season of long rains and we'd heard reports of a heavy downpour with floods in different parts of the city. To minimize incidents of drowning, the authorities were advising people to take caution. I had mixed feelings about this and was wondering if drowning in the floods would be a better option than continuing my life of abuse and insults with Akawd.

"I hope you don't get the wrong impression when I say this. I wasn't a fragile little girl who couldn't handle rough play, nor was I naïve about the existence of physical abuse in intimate relationships. I had grown up in the inner city where bullying and abuse was a part of life. I just didn't expect it in my own relationship, from someone I loved and had entrusted my life to. This should never have occurred in the safety of my own home, a home where God was acknowledged. Absolutely not. In my home, we would practice faith in Him and His Word.

"I knew how to defend myself, but I didn't want the situation to deteriorate to that level. I wasn't going to allow our home to become a battleground where parents solved their differences through verbal and physical assaults while the needs of the children were relegated to the background. Therefore, I decided to give faith a chance and allow God's wisdom to override the situation.

"On the morning of the heavy rains, I mentioned to my brother-in-law that I was going to go for a walk with the children through the torrent to clear my mind. I intentionally mentioned the possibility of drowning, saying, 'If we don't make it back home tonight, don't bother looking for us, because we might be victims of the flood.' It was a passive aggressive response, to make the point that there was a limit to what I could take. Akawd must have wondered why I was taking the children with me in the heavy downpour, but he didn't say a word. He could tell I wasn't looking for his or anyone's opinion or approval.

"Carrying my children, one wrapped around my back and the other fastened to my chest, I left the house and walked for one hour to my father's home. We were drenched and cold on arrival but happy to find my father there along with two of my siblings. One of my siblings made us tea with scones while the other entertained the children. The day slipped by more quickly than I would have preferred. Soon it was evening and I had to pack my children up and head back.

"Much as I would have liked to tell someone about the events of the previous night, to get it off my chest, I couldn't do that with my family. I was older than my siblings and by default a parental figure to them. My father was in his late fifties, a stage in life when it was expected that parents would relinquish their responsibilities to their adult children. It would have been devastating to show any weakness or signs of instability. So, to maintain my "good daughter" image, I did what I knew best; I kept everything to myself and returned home.

CHAPTER FIVE: PHYSICAL ABUSE

"The long walk home gave me ample time to reflect. The negative effects of the sporadic physical abuse I was suffering were becoming more and more obvious. They were threatening the very life of our relationship. I just wished that Akawd could see it, too. It was like a slow death, causing scars without stopping the heartbeat.

"Over the next ten years, I consistently called Akawd out on his behaviour. One day I made a statement that seemed to catch his attention. I told him, 'One day I'll be strong enough to stand up to you and stop you.' I had picked up some helpful self-defence techniques in the tough neighbourhood where I'd grown up, although I'd never thought I would need to defend myself from a loved one. I could never consider defending myself physically against Akawd, but he paid attention to the threat. I wanted him to know how much the abuse was hurting me, our relationship, and our family.

"Akawd would express remorse after each episode of abuse and beg forgiveness, but the cycle continued. At some point, I stood my ground and said, 'Enough.' It wasn't a one-time incident but a shift in the landscape of the family. We were living away from home now, in a foreign country where resources were scarce, and it was very important to maintain a healthy and stable family environment. We didn't have the luxury of the support of our extended families. We were just beginning to connect with a new community and to identify the spiritual and social supports available to us.

"Life away from home can bring with it unique challenges. As a family, we required safety and stability to navigate our way through it all and maximize our opportunities for growth and development. I reasoned with Akawd, helping him to see that the physical abuse was causing irreparable damage to the relationship and the children. He made a vow to work on his issues and find other, more constructive ways to address his frustration.

"This reprieve felt like a form of resuscitation, giving our relationship new life. He gave me his word and followed through with action. He promised to never lay his hand on me or any member of the family ever again. He had every intention of keeping that word—and for the most part, he did keep it.

"Unfortunately, Akawd chose to redirect his frustrations through another damaging channel—verbal abuse. Although he managed to exercise physical restraint, he couldn't curb his tongue. He had grown up in an environment where people settled their differences by hurling hurtful words at each other. He had learned this from the adults in his life. What he didn't realize, however, was that the verbal assaults inflicted a different kind of hurt—emotional and psychological hurt.

"But that can be a story for another day. I don't want to tire you with such a sad story. How about we end on something positive and pick up the topic of emotional abuse next time you visit?"

It was late in the evening, and I offered to stay later, but we both had to be at work the next day. Besides, I could tell that Muka was exhausted. So I offered to return later in the week, and she accepted.

I drove back home feeling grateful for the opportunity to have been a source of support for my friend.

My husband was still up waiting for me when I got home. He seemed worried, but I reassured him that all was well. He knew some of the story regarding our friends, but not all of it. He didn't press for details, although he asked if he could help in any way.

We both prayed for Muka and Akawd before retiring to bed.

CHAPTER SIX
EMOTIONAL AND PSYCHOLOGICAL ABUSE

The week rolled by pretty fast and I had plans that weekend. However, I rescheduled with Muka and called her to find out what time would work best for a follow-up visit. She proposed the following Friday afternoon. That date seemed to work well for both of us, and we could even make it an overnight visit. Given that this was to be a long weekend, I figured we would have ample time to get through the rest of story at a comfortable pace.

Coincidentally, we had a women's fellowship meeting scheduled for that weekend, on Saturday, but I didn't expect that Muka was planning to attend. I even offered to forego the fellowship and spend that time with her instead.

My husband and I spent the following week cleaning up the house and revamping the garden. Before long, the week had come and gone and Friday was upon us. I ran some errands that morning, and then proceeded to Muka's house by late afternoon with some Kenyan food I'd cooked for super. I'd also made some flat bread to which she added some green grams stew.

As we shared the meal, Muka recapped the story so far.

"My mother used to have a saying, one she repeated often: 'A wound too painful, but it does not bleed.' She said this regularly to convey that an emotional trauma can be subtle but just as painful, if not more so, than a physical trauma. It's a wound not immediately visible to the physical eye, but present in the mind. I believe my mother used this phrase to instruct my siblings and me about the damaging effects of all forms of verbal abuse.

"I tried to make Akawd understand that his verbal assaults were having a negative effect on me and our relationship, but my message didn't seem to reach him. Either my methods were ineffective or he just didn't get it. I was continually nursing wounds caused by his hurtful words, insults, name-calling, and false accusations. The damage was real. With every verbal assault, it felt like our love was strained beyond its capacity.

"After hearing some conversations between Akawd and his brother about their family history, I realized that verbal abuse had partially formed them into the people they were today. Even though this knowledge helped me understand and make sense of what was happening, it didn't make the emotional and psychological hurt any less painful.

"You see, I was raised in an environment that reinforced respect for others and discouraged any form of verbal abuse. My father had taken disciplinary measures against me and my siblings whenever we uttered negative words. There had been zero tolerance for name-calling and heated arguments in our house. When we fought, both the culprit and the victim were disciplined equally. Younger siblings were expected to take the high road and remove themselves from potential conflicts. If the younger sibling believed he or she was in the right, they still had to leave and allow the situation to cool off. They were then required to seek the intervention of an adult or another older sibling.

"We were forbidden from engaging in heated verbal exchanges with our siblings, especially older siblings. There was little to no room for disrespect, dishonouring others, or causing a scene. This is not to imply that our family was perfect or above reproach. In fact, there were many occasions when my father dispensed discipline. It was an ongoing process of instilling in us positive values and good behaviour.

CHAPTER SIX: EMOTIONAL AND PSYCHOLOGICAL ABUSE

"So yes, I understood that Akawd and I had very different upbringings. However, the psychological and emotional toll was sometimes too heavy for me. I attempted to offset the damage as much as I could, but nothing ever seemed to be enough. And the thing that bothered me most was the fact that we were both leaders in our church. I would have thought that adhering to our faith practices would have trumped his volatile past, and I still hoped this would happen at some point. I desired to raise our children according to our religious principles and the teachings we espoused and encouraged others to follow.

"Akawd seemed insecure and unsure of the stability of our relationship. It's possible that my stance didn't help much, since I came across as self-confident, according to my own upbringing. I was loyal and trusting to those who earned my trust and could be cautious and guarded with those outside that circle of trust.

"By the time Akawd and I had started our courtship, I was in my late teens and in no hurry to get married or settle down. Akawd was in his early twenties and felt like he was ready to settle down and raise a family. But whenever Akawd brought up the topic of marriage, I deferred, saying that it was too soon to think that. I believe he was frustrated, and he may even have misinterpreted my deferrals as a lack of commitment.

"I realize now that it's possible I didn't do enough to reassure him of my commitment. I just assumed that my word was enough. Even now, as I reflect on it, I cannot state with certainty that a different approach would have made a difference. What I suspect is that our different personalities and approaches compounded Akawd's insecurities.

"I made so many assumptions. I thought that Akawd's insecurities would subside after the wedding, but they didn't. He was suspicious of many of the interactions I had with other people in my life, whether in personal or professional contexts. I had an outgoing personality and have been described as a natural leader. I had been a group leader in school as early as my primary education days and I'd served on student councils both in college and at graduate school.

"Yes, I had always been a leader. After finishing college, I worked in the classroom as a kindergarten teacher before transitioning into Christian service. There, I served in and led children's programs. To work with young people, one has to develop an adventurous personality, which I did, and I continued working with youth after Akawd and I settled down into family life. I even facilitated and led women's fellowship meetings as I matured into adulthood. I was known for my confidence and strong interpersonal skills.

"I should also mention that I worked in a male-dominated environment. Akawd was always suspicious about it and he insinuated that my colleagues were interested in me. He demanded that I give lengthy and detailed accounts of my days at work. Sometimes he even told me to recount the details of meetings which he already knew about, as a test of my loyalty. It felt like I was constantly under scrutiny. He cast his suspicions in every direction, at my colleagues, friends, acquaintances, and even our fellow church leaders. The situation produced unending psychological stress.

"I once asked Akawd why he didn't have faith in the goodness of humanity. After all, although some people exist who have insincere intentions, most people aren't like that. He tended to suspect everyone and seemed to dwell too much on the pessimistic side of life, questioning everything and everyone, doubting every intention.

"I attempted to understand his over-the-top distrust. It turned out, once again, that his early life accounted for it, including instances of infidelity, distrust, and backstabbing by those supposedly within his circle of trust. His aunt had told tales of unfaithful spouses, mainly women, and cautioned young men to never trust their spouses. In his own family, there was a long-running debate about one member of the family's paternity.

"However, our faith was based on the foundation of trust. I adhered to scriptural teachings that demanded absolute fidelity to God the Most High, the Father of all created beings. I reassured Akawd constantly that my respect and fidelity to him as my spouse and to my family was based on my love and respect for God and His commandments. I also reiterated that this wasn't dependent on his attempts to police my life or place unreasonable expectations and demands on me. I believed, and still believe, that any other basis for fidelity and trust is likely to fall short. Even though I felt insulted that Akawd thought so low of me, I

CHAPTER SIX: EMOTIONAL AND PSYCHOLOGICAL ABUSE

defended myself over and over when he expressed suspicion or doubted my accounts.

"It was humiliating, but I didn't hold this behaviour against Akawd. I forgave him even though he never asked for forgiveness or felt the need to ask for it. I held on to the hope that someday Akawd would realize that I was totally and completely committed to him. Maybe he would eventually learn to relax. But that hope was never to be realized. In the end, it was yet another demeaning and insulting allegation that caused him to walk out on me.

"The best I could do was let Akawd know that I didn't appreciate his methods of conflict resolution. There was no way for me to enforce my values on him. In keeping with my cultural ideals, I opted to respond in a passive aggressive manner, which didn't always work. Indeed, the cost of this approach was high. I tolerated a lot. Although these assaults debilitated our relationship, my decision to remain tolerant protected our relationship, even offering it a reprieve. We kept the relationship going, even though we were emotionally depleted. For a while, I thought that love and forgiveness had triumphed. There seemed to be enough love and forgiveness to return our relationship to good health."

It was getting late into the evening when Muka trailed off, and she proposed that we take a break. We listened to worship songs, sang along, then shared a prayer and retired to bed for the night.

Muka had offered me the guest room downstairs, which provided a cool and comfortable environment for sleep. Even though my body was tired, my mind was fully awake, actively processing Muka's story.

In particular, I wondered about her thoughts on love and forgiveness. Had love and forgiveness failed her? Like an overprescribed medication, they seemed to have become less and less effective over time in treating the ailments that plagued the marriage.

I felt so helpless that night and said another prayer for my friend. I prayed that the process of sharing her story would be as helpful for her as it was for me. I was gaining so much insight just by listening.

I finally drifted into a deep sleep.

CHAPTER SEVEN
FINANCES

I meant to wake up early and make breakfast for both of us on Saturday morning. However, I received a phone call from my husband, who was on a weekend expedition up north with his friends. He had wanted to check on me and reassure me that he was praying for both of us. The call took a while, and by the time we were done talking I discovered that Muka had already put breakfast on the table.

Muka said she was glad that my husband had called, because she too had planned to get up early and prepare breakfast ready for us. We said our morning prayers and then sat down for the meal.

Muka checked again to confirm whether I was okay to listen to her story, and I confirmed that I was. She seemed so relieved, because the next part of the story was going to be hard for her to divulge. She was reluctant to discuss the topic of finances, and I assured her that it would be okay for her to skip it. However, she felt this had been a major component in the breakdown of the marriage.

After that brief check-in, she picked up the story again.

"My reluctance in discussing our finances is based on the fact that we served in non-profit, faith-based institutions that depend on donations. We worked to develop ourselves on a personal and professional level, not necessarily to increase our income. We had expected that our income would often be uncertain. As such, we had to be keen and effective managers of our meagre resources. We were supported by the fellowships we served and, for the most part, lived from hand to mouth.

"The first congregation we served in, early in our marriage, was located in a large slum where most of the residents were either unemployed or depended on casual labour. The church members' support couldn't effectively meet the needs of the congregation, not to mention sustain our young family, so I secured a teaching position in a private kindergarten that paid well and held that position for over a year. That opportunity served our family in more ways than one. Our older child began her early childhood education in that school. In the meantime, Akawd was completing his graduate studies in one of the city's leading theological institutions. This gave us enough income to meet our basic needs and provide for our young family.

"Needless to say, our financial situation required us to engage in prudent financial planning. Financial management is a tough skill to master, even for those who have enough resources to afford some comfort. Akawd would jokingly say that I was the Minister of Finance in our household. He acknowledged that the nifty-gritty details of budgeting, planning, and distributing resources challenged him. His best efforts put our account in the red month after month. He addressed this by getting an overdraft protection plan.

"However, further challenges arose when Akawd's financial situation improved after we settled in Canada. He desired to resume the development and evangelism projects he had started back home in his village. For most of his adult life, Akawd had nourished a deep concern for those who lived in rural areas and weren't able to afford a decent life. He now endeavoured to set aside funds and commit them to programs that could make a difference in people's lives. Despite his best efforts, though, these projects progressed much more slowly than he expected.

"Even though these various financial demands exceeded Akawd's financial resources, living abroad offered him the illusion of wealth in terms of being able to access credit. Akawd found himself time and again tripping into nasty financial holes and needed to be lifted out. He

CHAPTER SEVEN: FINANCES

revived existing projects and initiated new ones, kept an unnecessary list of staff and overextended himself. Our already staggering mortgage constantly had to absorb his debts. He always promised to get rid of his multiple credit cards, but the promise was never kept. Once the debt was absorbed, the cycle would just begin again.

"I came up with an idea to remedy the situation. I opened a separate account and directed the income from my second job into it as a saving scheme. The income from my main employment continued to flow into the joint account. I also proposed that we come up with a plan that would distribute funds to cover our household needs; I would take care of bills and recurring expenses and Akawd would take care of the monthly mortgage. Akawd countered that I should pay the mortgage while he covered bills and expenses. I was ready and willing to take either one of these financial obligations, but Akawd's counterproposal was just a delaying tactic. I transferred funds into the joint account to cover mortgage payments for the month, but Akawd didn't direct the funds needed to pay the bills. The bills happened to have been registered to my new account, so I proceeded to pay them all.

"Akawd made a big fuss out of the situation, insisting that my plan was skewed against him. Despite my attempt to itemize every amount, thereby demonstrating to him that the total figure for paying the bills was higher than the figure needed to pay the mortgage, he still believed that he was getting a raw deal. It took prolonged discussions and arguments for Akawd to finally accept the plan, albeit reluctantly.

"The plan distributed financial responsibilities equally between the two of us. It enabled me to begin narrowing the gap on our overdrafts. Akawd also decided to open a separate account for his income and monitor the funds more effectively. He did transfer the mortgage payments into the joint account, but I didn't feel comfortable with my decision to have a separate account. However, his financial ineptitude led him to make poor choices.

"To his credit, Akawd did suggest that we go back to directing all of our income into the joint account. Under normal circumstances, that would have been the reasonable thing to do. However, Akawd had demonstrated a lack of financial competence so I stood my ground, not wanting to return to the poor financial management that had left our joint account permanently in the red. All I wanted was to get our financial situation back on solid ground. Since I couldn't convince him to do it, my only option was to keep our accounts separated.

"This new state of affairs may have addressed our ongoing financial maladies, but it didn't help our relationship. Healthy finances are a marker for a healthy relationship, and I tend to agree that couples will benefit from maintaining a unified financial stance and exercise full transparency with each other. So I was conflicted about the decision to separate our accounts. It went against what I had counselled other couples to do.

"But it was impossible to practice prudent financial management with Akawd's unrelenting spending. Even with his new account, Akawd maintained an overdraft status and was always transferring funds back and forth between the various accounts to keep things moving. Meanwhile, his projects back in Africa continued, and even expanded, yet his financial resources remained the same. His need to borrow money grew over time. Akawd believed that he had to invest in the projects to get them started and that they would later attract the necessary capital to continue. The projects included developing and training personnel to spearhead initiatives like education, healthcare, and income-generating schemes. He acquired small properties from families or acquaintances and recruited people to oversee construction. It was a challenging and complicated endeavour to coordinate remotely.

"These were the kinds of challenges Akawd faced and insisted on attempting to overcome. By the end, his projects were left incomplete and buildings were either condemned or fraudulently taken over by those who had been tasked with constructing them. The consequences for our family's finances were devastating, made worse by the fact that this came at a time when Akawd's main source of stable income came to an end when he was laid off by the company he was working for.

"Before he was laid off, Akawd took out an even bigger loan so that he could go back to the village and jumpstart his ailing projects. He hadn't been able to get approval for such a loan on his own income, so he'd asked me to co-sign the loan with our mortgage as collateral.

CHAPTER SEVEN: FINANCES

Understandably, I was cautious and tried to explain that it didn't seem to be a sound plan. I pleaded with Akawd to reconsider, but it didn't go well.

"When I decided not to give in to him, he settled for a lesser loan that the bank could approve without my signature or the mortgage as a security, although this loan came with a higher interest rate. He did travel back to Africa, though, and acquired a bigger and more economically viable property in an urban area to relocate his projects. This didn't end well. He fell victim to a shrewd would-be partner to whom he handed over everything. He was left with nothing but a laptop, his personal documents, and the clothes he was wearing. These losses had far-reaching implications. His reputation suffered a major setback and most of his associates walked away to reconsider their support. He returned home feeling defeated.

"Even after this devastating experience, though, Akawd still believed that more money would solve his problems. He wanted to take out yet another loan. Unfortunately, my answer was still no—this time with a capital N. In protest, he threatened to stop making the mortgage payments. I had suspected this was coming and was prepared to assume the mortgage and all our financial responsibilities. He followed through on his threat and began pouring all his money into his projects. His long-term plan was to relocate back to Africa, assume responsibility for the projects, and redirect his time and effort to make it work. Meanwhile, I committed myself to protecting our family home and adjusted the household budget to survive on one income."

"Saying no to this last request for a big loan seems to have been among the final stressors in the relationship. Akawd declared that I wasn't being supportive of him. He had made that accusation many times before, especially when things weren't going well for him. I just explained my position, saying that his job was ending and we needed to take prudent financial steps to prepare for the coming transition to one income. I recommended that he take the time to reassess his financial priorities and salvage whatever he could from his projects. That's when Akawd declared the marriage dissolved."

Muka paused in her tale, taking a few moments to gather herself.

"I didn't take him seriously, but at least I made the symbolic gesture of moving out of the bedroom and sleeping on the couch for a week," she continued. "Akawd then apologized profusely for making that statement. He begged me to bring my belongings back to the bedroom and asked for forgiveness. Again, I believed that we had enough love and forgiveness to redeem the relationship. I thought that love and forgiveness had come through again and rescued us."

At this point, I gently interjected to express my surprise at how deftly she had handled the situation.

"Well, I had gotten used to his temper tantrums," she said. "I had always hoped he would outgrow them in the course of time, but he never seemed to. I couldn't understand why. Why couldn't he comprehend that such behaviours were destructive? At least my spiritual resilience remained a source of support for me. It enabled me to tolerate what was happening to us."

CHAPTER EIGHT
SPIRITUAL RESILIENCE

After breakfast, I helped clear the table. Then Muka led the way to the living room again, where we settled down on the couch with our drinks. I knew what was coming next and was very eager to hear more about Muka's spiritual resilience. It would help me to understand the source of her strength and learn from her experience and wisdom. I couldn't imagine going through something as traumatic as what she had endured. How was she able to cope?

The narrative proceeded without interruption.

"The various abuses and financial problems exerted considerable strain on the relationship," Muka said. "I also battled bouts of depression. Still, my spirit remained strong and resilient. I had resolved early in the relationship to protect my spiritual wellness from all these maladies. By the grace of God, I succeeded. My faith was a vibrant aspect of my life and it had sustained me over the years. If anything, the challenges caused me to reaffirm my belief in God and place things in a proper perspective. I reoriented my mind to things of eternal value and spiritual wealth.

"I believed all along that I had the will power and the resources I needed to protect my spiritual life from the effects of abuse. This contributed greatly to the inner strength and balance that characterized my life, and I strived to do my best to pass on my faith to our children. Knowing that Akawd's approach to life had the potential to hamper the course of our children's growth and development, I compensated as much as possible. The same faith that had worked in me and kept me from crumbling had the potential to sustain our children as they navigated the mucky waters of life. I wanted to provide a better environment for them, an environment with two healthy and functional parents. The least I could do was ground them in faith and connect them with God. I purposed not to allow the negative dynamics in our household to derail my efforts to provide an environment that fostered spiritual growth and well-being. I did this by modelling a lifestyle of prayer and dependence on God.

"For me, theology and faith aren't just a lifestyle, they are life. Knowing and loving God is the air that sustains me. I can't imagine going one day, not even one hour, without the life sustaining Word and presence of God. If I were to quote some of the scriptures that have sustained me, I would end up quoting the whole Bible. It is sufficient to say that the Word of God kept me safe, encouraging and empowering me for good works. As 2 Corinthians 9:8 says, *'And God is able to make all grace abound toward you, that you, always having all sufficiency in all things, may have an abundance for every good work.'* Proverbs 4:23 admonishes us, *'Keep your heart with all diligence, for out of it spring the issues of life.'* I believed and acted on God's Word with confidence. I credit my spiritual resilience to my personal faith in God and the grounding that my church gave me by teaching the *'whole counsel of God'* (Acts 20:27).

"In addition to being raised on biblical principles by a father who believed and practiced God's Word, I was also fortunate to commit my life to God at a very young age. I was given a positive start in life thanks to the teachings of the Christian faith and a parent who believed and lived out the principles outlined in the Bible. In the process of life, I committed myself to the pursuit of faith before I reached adolescence. My youthful years were centred on the church and serving in its programs, including Christian education, small group sessions, Sunday school lessons, singing in the choir, and participating in youth activities.

These opportunities afforded me a holistic grounding in physical, mental, social, and spiritual maturity.

"If I were to pinpoint the source of my resilience, it would definitely include the words of Ephesians 1:3: *'Blessed be the God and Father of our Lord Jesus Christ, who has blessed us with every spiritual blessing in the heavenly places in Christ.'* Despite my circumstances, I have always had the assurance that God reserves for me the spiritual resources I need in life, and they include spiritual blessings that supersede my physical needs. I would trade every worldly pleasure for the comfort of spiritual blessings. I know that I am eternally safe and secure in God. With this assurance, I was able to accept my situation and focus on what I had the ability to change within the relationship.

"I also sought out opportunities for professional development, both to advance myself and maintain my sanity. Some opportunities for respite included leadership in an interdenominational organization that coordinated annual family camps and retreats, as well as leading an ongoing initiative to bring together women of faith. Speaking of which, we do have a fellowship to get to later today, don't we?"

I was so consumed by Muka's story that for a moment I didn't even understand the question.

In any event, Muka continued without waiting for an answer. "You see, the work of this women's fellowship has been a positive influence in my life. It started as a grassroots initiative of women from different ethnic communities who had one thing in common: faith. I was called upon to provide leadership in the fellowship and other similar groups. These opportunities have provided avenues for me to engage in spiritually refreshing moments that make my marital problems more bearable.

"To be fair, I should clarify that our relationship hasn't been in a constant state of crisis, as I've made it sound. There have been moments of happiness. And yet... well, I know you haven't asked, but in case you're thinking it... yes, I've come to see that loving and marrying Akawd was a mistake. But it's a mistake I don't regret, for many reasons. For one thing, I've had the opportunity to experience a less than ideal human love against the backdrop of the perfect and all-embracing love of God. Another reason, the biggest reason, is that I've had the wonderful privilege of becoming a mother to our loving, patient, and committed children. Maybe that sounds selfish. Perhaps they could still have been born into this world even if we hadn't been their parents. They would have had slightly different forms, of course, and maybe they would have had parents who did a better job than Akawd and I could ever do. My biggest regret is that my children received a raw deal in life. However, my love and dedication to them and their well-being is beyond measure. I love them to pieces, and will always regret that this story has become their legacy, too."

With that, Muka insisted that we stop in order to attend that evening's meeting. It was almost midday already and the fellowship was scheduled to begin by 4:00 p.m. But first Muka rose and proposed that we listen to some worship music. We danced right there in the middle of her kitchen.

The drive to the fellowship took about two hours, and she suggested that she would finish the last part of the story on the way. But first we had to make some snacks to share with the other women at the meeting.

CHAPTER NINE
THE FINAL BLOW

I offered to drive, but Muka insisted on sitting behind the wheel. She explained that she found driving to be therapeutic, especially on the weekends.

"I also don't want to put you in a difficult position if I say something surprising while we're on the highway," she said. "I've already lived my story, so I know what's coming, but you don't."

I gladly obliged and so we departed.

"Any one of the issues I've mentioned so far had the potential to harm our marriage," she said as we pulled out onto the road. "After talking it through, it seems obvious to me now that each problem contributed to the breakdown of the relationship. I had hoped all along that our relationship would continue on and even improve, perhaps with the help of counselling, which would give us room to address our challenges and focus on our strengths. After all, I think we still have strong reasons to remain together—common interest, a long history, thriving children, and now growing grandchildren. But it wasn't meant to be. The events of the last two years have demonstrated just how much the relationship has deteriorated. We came to the point where any small misunderstanding could easily devolve into a major argument.

"The final blow came a little while ago when Akawd tried to manufacture a crisis, accusing me of an unforgivable deed that would blow my life and reputation to pieces. He was convinced that I had committed a heinous act to destroy our relationship, our family, and my reputation. Understandably, I was confused. I couldn't figure out exactly what transgression I was supposedly guilty of this time around, given that I had already defended myself against multiple accusations in the past.

"I was getting tired of always pleading my case. Almost every accusation Akawd made against me stemmed from him misinterpreting my actions or words. In each case, I went to great lengths to explain myself so that he could better understand the situation and consider withdrawing the accusation. However, with every new accusation he made references to past ones. It felt like my life was being played out in a courtroom where Akawd was the prosecutor, the judge, the jury, and the key witness.

"Allow me to illustrate this with an example. For most of my adult life until arriving in Canada, and even during my early years as an immigrant, I've served in a male-dominated profession. In the early nineties, I was a graduate school administrator. One among my duties was serving on the school's administrative committee, which consisted mostly of men. One evening, I came home from an afternoon meeting and he asked how my day had been.

"'Long,' I said. 'But good.'

"'What did you do today?'

"'The usual. Admin work in the morning and a meeting in the afternoon.'

"'What kind of meeting?'

"'An administrative committee meeting.'

"'Who was there?'

"'All the committee members.'

"Then his interrogation got more specific, and he asked if the head of the department had attended the meeting—which of course he had.

"'Where did he sit at the table?' Akawd asked next.

"'Actually, he sat right beside me.'

CHAPTER NINE: THE FINAL BLOW

"'Who arrived first at the meeting... you or him?'

"'I did.'

"'Is there a reason he sat beside you?'

"I hesitated for a moment, thinking about my answer. 'The only reason I can come up with is that the seat was empty.'

"'Was there no other empty seat?'

"Once again, I had to think back. 'There were three other empty seats. People were still filing in.'

"'So there were four empty seats, but he chose the seat beside you.'

"'Yeah, I guess he did. There's nothing strange about that.'

"'You don't see it, do you?'

"'See what?'

"'He's interested in you!' Akawd said, raising his voice. 'And the fact that you don't see it means you are either in denial or you like the attention. Which one is it?'

"'That's absurd. I can give you more than ten reasons to dispute that theory. Key among them, he's a Christian and a married man. But even if neither one of those things were true, you still wouldn't need to be concerned. He'd be wasting his time.'

"'So you say. I just want you to be careful around him. I saw how he was conducting himself around you.'

"Suddenly it dawned on me that Akawd was asking about something he already knew about. Apparently he'd had a clear view of the meeting and just wanted to see if I would lie about it. In his own twisted way, he was playing the investigator. There were many such incidents during our marriage. It would take weeks just to retell half the incidents, but this one is a perfect example of what my life had become.

"As for the final blow I was talking about, the most recent allegation Akawd levelled against me, which I couldn't understand, played out in much the same way. He accused me of infidelity and claimed that he had hard proof this time and I couldn't talk myself out of it. Knowing I had not engaged, and could never have dreamed of engaging, in such despicable behaviour, I dismissed his accusation and chose not to entertain it. I had learned over the years to protect my soul and peace of mind by dismissing such accusations while also defending myself. It was very important that I not allow such delusional allegations to get me down. So I did what I had always done—I denied it and went on with my regular routines and responsibilities.

"However, what made this final allegation interesting was that it came about at the exact time that Akawd was losing his job again. Not surprisingly, this was going to make his financial situation very difficult. I asked myself, was he having a midlife crisis or perhaps a bout of depression? But he continued with the accusation, adding new information each time. He hinted at having evidence of my indiscretion in the form of a recording on his phone. I pleaded with him to show me the evidence, but he wouldn't do it. I wasn't worried about proving my innocence, since I hadn't done anything; I was worried that he had fabricated something and was about to use it against me.

"Indeed, Akawd had shared this information with lots of people—his immediate family, his acquaintances, and his colleagues and associates. Apparently these people had known about the allegations for months and not one of them had shown the courage to bring it to my attention. I had no idea that these allegations had been communicated to such a large number of people, including our mutual friends. I had believed that I was succeeding in keeping it under wraps.

"I even offered to take a polygraph test for the purpose of helping clear the air. Akawd did not seem interested in that. Finally, I said to him, 'Do you have evidence to back this up? You sound very convincing, yet I know for a fact that I have done no such thing.' To my surprise, he used that very statement months later to scoff at me, saying, 'I got you this time. You challenged me by saying I didn't have any evidence, but now I do and you're finished.' How had Akawd come to believe that he had evidence of my non-existent infidelity? It was quite a perplexing situation. The sort of thing you might expect to see in a movie.

"Akawd was about to travel back home to Africa, so I insisted that we at least speak with a counsellor, or our pastor, about the allegations and seek some resolution. Akawd refused this request, informing me that he didn't want to expose me to anyone. In desperation, I threatened to involve law enforcement if he didn't release this so-called

CHAPTER NINE: THE FINAL BLOW

evidence before leaving the country. He said he didn't want to have this evidence analyzed by people who didn't speak or understand our language.

"I was invested in clearing my name not because I thought Akawd deserved it at this late stage in our marriage, but because I suspected Akawd might not be in his right mind. Therefore, I insisted on one last option, which he accepted as a reasonable compromise. I proposed the option of inviting a mutual friend to review the evidence, someone Akawd trusted. So we called someone we knew, an engineer who had twice joined us for singing events in the neighbourhood."

It turned out that I knew this person.

"Did it help?" I asked.

"Well, Akawd was to release the evidence in the presence of this individual and he would then help determine its authenticity. I have to admit, I felt both relieved and insulted at the same time. Relieved that I would finally have the chance to clear my name in the presence of a witness, and insulted that I actually had to do this at all, witness or not.

"When I called the individual, I first apologized to him, guilt-stricken that we were about to ask him to do this. I then explained why we needed him and asked if he would be available to join us. He kindly made time out of his busy schedule to help with this embarrassing task and stopped by our house one Sunday evening. Akawd was resting at home, his employment having ended by this time. He was making final plans for what was to be an extended trip home.

"We invited our friend into the house and Akawd brought out his phone and laptop to play a recording. He insisted that this was the proof that I had broken our marriage vows and given him a reason to leave the relationship. Needless to say, I didn't believe the recording would show any indiscretion. How could it? No indiscretion had occurred.

"What we heard was a recording of a television program with very poor audio. After two hours of repeatedly playing it to convince this witness and myself that the recording was indeed actual evidence of my infidelity, the individual needed to leave. He made one more appeal to Akawd, asking him to consider that he could be wrong. Akawd was furious at this suggestion and went on a tirade, accusing me of all sorts of unethical behaviour. He used words I would never feel comfortable repeating to anyone, much less to a friend.

"Our friend seemed visibly distraught and asked to be excused. Before leaving, though, he added, 'Let us pretend for a moment that there *is* evidence of indiscretion and that Muka has indeed betrayed you. I would still beg you to reconsider your next step. Do not break your family over this. Be a leader and show compassion.'

"It was a pathetic scene. I was on my knees, sobbing in disbelief at all the things Akawd had said about me in the presence of our mutual friend. I had hoped to be exonerated, but instead I ended up being crushed beyond my wildest imagination. Akawd seemed really pleased with himself, too. He withdrew to the bedroom, a room I had moved out of to take refuge in one of the children's rooms, and started making phone calls. I learned later that Akawd was calling his family and friends back home to update them on recent events. From his perspective, I had been busted and called out in my indiscretion and was crying in shame and guilt. My defences had fallen flat and I had no one to blame but myself. Akawd was celebrating his soon-coming freedom from his life with me—a life he was about to begin sharing with a new partner, as I would discover."

At this point, Muka paused for a while to catch her breath. I asked if she was okay to continue driving, and she confirmed that she was. We were about halfway into the trip to the women's fellowship meeting.

"I called my brother back home," Muka said, continuing the tale. "We debriefed, then prayed together on the phone amidst my sobs. Following that phone conversation and prayer, I decided to leave for the night. I packed a twenty-four-hour emergency backpack and left to spend the night at the home of one of our adult children. I made that decision out of concern for my safety. For the first time, I was truly gripped with fear. I was both afraid of what Akawd would do next and also worried that he was unstable. I didn't believe it was safe to be alone with him in the house that night.

"As you know, it's uncommon in our culture for a woman my age to move in with her daughter, even for a temporary stay. That's how desperate I was that night. She invited me to their guest room, but I insisted on sleeping on the couch—or at least I tried to sleep.

CHAPTER NINE: THE FINAL BLOW

"I woke up very early in the morning, before my daughter and her family were up, packed my backpack, and left for work. My plan was to arrange to take some time off so I could find a new place to live for a little while. Thankfully, my supervisor not only understood but also went out of his way to help me. Someone I knew had a missionary apartment that just happened to be available. I moved in for the next two weeks, the length of time before Akawd was scheduled to travel to Africa.

"I had hoped that the time away would give Akawd some much-needed respite and that he would perceive things more clearly after spending time with his family. I even hoped that his family members would hear his delusional allegations and set him straight. But I chose not to mention any of these allegations to them in advance, in an effort not to influence their reaction to Akawd during his visit. I even expected to receive word from some of them, seeking to understand what Akawd was reporting to them. But that didn't happen. When I did make calls to inquire about what Akawd had been telling people, I learned that he was saying that I had walked out on him. The family was in a state of disbelief. Many of them didn't believe these allegations while others didn't know what to believe. I didn't have a strong enough command of Akawd's first language to explain myself to them. I usually depended on him to translate messages and facilitate our conversations, which obviously wouldn't be possible anymore.

"Well, eventually I caught on to the full effect of what was taking place: Akawd had pretty much moved on. I discovered that he already had a new partner in Africa, and together they had acquired a new property with the loan he had secured. Learning this, I took steps to protect myself by blocking his access to any of my accounts and to the house.

"To make a long story short, his new relationship quickly fell apart, he lost the property, and had to cut his trip short. When he got back to the house, I demanded that he see a doctor. Instead he just stayed away and insisted that I buy him out of our house. I didn't take him seriously, just as I hadn't taken him seriously in the past. I must have been in denial, because he had entered yet another relationship by this point and was planning a wedding. Within a few months, he served me divorce papers and entered bankruptcy protection to make sure he got his portion of our assets. With the bankruptcy, he surrendered his ownership of the property to a bankruptcy trustee. I did my best to stop it all, to no avail.

"I tried to educate the trustee about our cultural practices, specifically the one that demands that a woman not be displaced from her home. He mocked this argument, saying that he couldn't operate under the laws or practices of another jurisdiction. So I appealed instead on the basis of reason. I tried to explain that I had invested all my savings in that property. Akawd's income had been inconsistent in all the years we'd lived there, meaning that I was principally responsible for the down-payment and mortgage instalments. Surely no good-hearted person would be willing to take the home from me! Well, the trustee wouldn't hear of it. He challenged me to try and take that argument to a judge, which I did try. At least, I ended up getting a bit of child support back. Doing all that with both a full-time and part-time job has proven challenging, to put it mildly.

"The fallout from all this has been devastating. It feels like he stabbed me right in the heart and twisted the knife, and I told him this. He seemed surprised to hear and simply replied that he was just trying to solve his financial problems. When he tried pressuring me to agree to the divorce, I refused. I didn't believe he was in the right state of mind to make such a life-altering decision. Besides, through consultations with legal experts, I learned that if I was to file for divorce while Akawd was unemployed, I would end up paying him spousal support. Akawd was aware of all this, but he didn't say anything. He was desperate to end the relationship and move on. Apparently there was a growing list of women ready to help nurse his broken heart back to health.

"When he finally did file for divorce, I made every effort to derail the process, although a lawyer told me that it would be futile. So it would seem that my husband Akawd, who set out to mould me into his idea of a perfect wife, decided to abandon me when that didn't work. Now he's going to make a new life, a new family for himself.

CHAPTER NINE: THE FINAL BLOW

"That brings us right to today. Now I'm just waiting for the courts to make a decision about a marriage they have no business making decisions about, except that Akawd has given them that power. It's ironic that he and I met in the church and sought the blessings of God. Now he prefers to abide by the decree of the courts, through a judge. But at least I've had this opportunity to place our relationship on the table, so to speak, to attempt to deconstruct the mystery behind our ailing relationship. Thank you. It is both a complicated and an ambiguous grief."

Muka sighed, paused for a moment, and then changed the subject.

"We're just a few minutes away," she said. "Maybe we should just drive the rest of the way in silence. Maybe you need a minute or two to reorient yourself."

I smiled. "Thanks for offering, but I should be good. It's you I'm worried about. Are you okay to proceed? I don't mind if we turn right around and drive back home."

"No, I'm fine. In fact, I need this fellowship. It will be good for my spirit to see everyone. And I think this will be the perfect distraction from all the chaos in my life right now."

Before long, we pulled into the driveway of the church and walked into a room filled with women ready to worship. The afternoon went well. We had a good time of fellowship over God's Word, and we shared some good food as well.

I kept my eyes on Muka throughout the meeting, just in case she would need my help. However, she seemed fine throughout the worship and into the social time.

Later, we said our goodbyes as people started to leave. We finally said farewell to the host team and headed out.

It was a quiet drive home. Muka turned on the radio and connected to a Christian station. We listened to some great worship songs together.

When we walked back into Muka's home, she assured me that she was okay.

"Thank you very much for your time and presence," she said in gratitude. "You've been very helpful. You're welcome to stay as long as you like, but I don't intend to ask any more of your time."

"It was an honour, Muka. I'm glad I could be here with you to listen. Please know that I'm just a phone call away… but I won't wait for you to call. If you let me, I'd like to check on you and pray with you through this process."

She accepted my offer.

We shared a prayer, and then I left. I felt much lighter in the spirit than I had upon coming to her house the previous day. As sad as the story was, Muka had managed to tell it in a warm and touching manner. I was glad she had invited me into her story and that we had shared the weekend.

CHAPTER TEN
IN A COMA

About six months later, I checked on Muka to ask how she was doing and find out if her and Akawd's divorce had been finalized. I had written down a draft of her story and wanted to give her chance to read it through.

It turned out that there had been an interesting twist. In the past half-year, Muka had taken a vacation to her home in Africa, a visit which she described as refreshing and nerve-wrecking at the same time. During the trip, she met with some members of Akawd's family and heard about Akawd's new partner, who had assumed the responsibility of caring for his mother.

Despite the mixed emotions evoked by the trip, Muka sounded cheerful when describing the positive support she'd received from her siblings, who were disappointed about what Akawd had done to their family.

"I asked all my siblings to keep this information from our parents, though," she said. "I would never dream of burdening them with such a story in their senior years. They deserve to live their final days in peace, not worrying about their children. They worried enough for us when we were growing up. It's our turn to do all the worrying."

Another thing Muka mentioned caught my attention. She had received a message from Akawd at the beginning of the year, on a busy mid-morning while at work. He'd explained that he had realized he had made a big mistake. He was sorry.

"What exactly does that mean?" I asked, registering surprise. I wasn't sure if I had heard her right. "What did he expect?"

"I cannot purport to know what Akawd is thinking, or what he hoped to accomplish with that message," she said, "but I know that I forgave him long before he even asked. I had to forgive—for my own health and well-being. You know, I never thought he had the capacity to take responsibility for his betrayal, but I wasn't sure if I could trust him. The last three years were so full of pain and sorrow. Even today, I'm still processing the effects of his actions.

"He sure did sound remorseful, though. He even admitted that he wasn't expecting to be allowed back in. 'I'm too tangled in my own mess to expect you to take me back,' he said. 'I just want you to know that I'm sorry.' The conversation only served to reassure me that he might still be capable of having feelings. But it didn't change the situation. His words sounded like the screeching of tires when a vehicle comes to a sudden stop. I held my breath, briefly, just to appreciate that we could have a somewhat normal-sounding conversation.

"Upon hearing him apologize, my mind ran with different possibilities. My first hypothesis was that Akawd had suffered a mental breakdown and was just coming out of it. But as much as I wanted to ask him questions and demand answers, I was still afraid to engage in a conversation with him, afraid that he would lash out and hurt my fragile emotions. If I let him do that to me again, the shame would rest squarely on my shoulders. So I ended the awkward conversation by simply letting him know that I had forgiven him.

"I wondered to myself, was Akawd just playing games with my emotions? Was he genuinely sorry? I had no way of knowing the truth, so I accepted the fact that I would never know. I chose to proceed with caution and focus on my new reality—life without Akawd. I had to admit that it would have been easier if he'd chosen to move to Africa and stayed there, but instead he decided to rebuild his life in the same region as me. I know that there are multiple versions of our story out there. The dominant one among our acquaintances is that I kicked him out of the house, and most people are too careful to ask for the story behind it.

"Now I'm beginning to settle into my new status—still married, in my eyes, but to a prodigal husband. I've rejected the label of ex-wife. The bankruptcy trustee was the first person to call me that—well, his actual words were 'disgruntled ex-wife.' At the time, he was disputing my claim on sole ownership of the house. All he wanted to do was safeguard the portion of the property Akawd had served him on a silver platter.

"I'm constructing a new story now, setting my family on an unfamiliar path, unaware of what we will become. The future is a moving target. I'm still working on what this all means for the structure of my family."

Finally, Muka asked me to share her story, in the hope that others might be able to learn from her sad tale. She didn't think she was the right one to tell the story, as she was too involved in it. Besides, she was still processing the fact that her marriage was essentially stuck in a coma, perhaps never to be revived.

"So, my friend, this is but a succinct version of my story," she concluded. "It's the brief summary of a marriage that now lies in a coma. He and I are still very much alive, but as for our marriage... well, death did us part."

I didn't get the impression that this experience had crushed Muka's spirit. On the contrary, she seemed stronger and more committed to her family than ever. She was maintaining her positive approach to life and continuing to be an inspiration to her peers.

I stayed in the loop regarding their divorce proceedings, but left the decision with Muka about how much she wanted to share with me. She had honoured me with her story and I held it in high regard. I decided to take the time to process everything she had told me.

CHAPTER ELEVEN
My Analysis

My latest conversation with Muka led me to conduct a critical exploration of my initial hypothesis that a marriage can end for other reasons beyond the death of one of the spouses; a marriage itself can die even if the two people living in it do not.

It seemed that Akawd had been having second thoughts about his decision to file for divorce, yet he had gotten himself too tangled in his own issues to make his way back. It's not clear if he had apologized because he actually meant it or because he had needed to soothe his conscience. Given everything he had said and done, I believed he could be found responsible for the marriage's end. At this point, all he and Muka were waiting for was the decree of a judge, and then it would be over.

But looking beyond the legal state of their marriage, I also had to consider the spiritual and cultural factors at play. What would happen if Akawd and Muka returned to their homes in Africa? In that culture, once a woman is married, her husband's home becomes her home. So where would Muka's home be? She no longer had a place of her own in her father's house.

And what would Akawd's status be? A divorce may be decreed in Canada by a judge, but would that divorce be recognized back home?

As an elder in his father's home and a leader in the community, what message would his behaviour communicate to his family and peers?

I chose to start by examining the role of faith and culture. In her narrative, Muka had revealed that she and Akawd had been friends before becoming a couple. They had enjoyed positive experiences together, connecting on the basis of their faith before viewing each other as possible life partners. They had cared for and respected each other as equals in their respective fields. Their romantic love had been built on a sound foundation of friendship and respect.

Based on this love, Muka had erroneously believed that only death could bring about an end to their marriage. She had believed this based on her love for Akawd and his reassurances of love for her. They had both made certain assumptions leading up to their marriage, and even in the early years of their marriage.

I now pondered three main questions:

- Was their relationship equipped with the resources it needed to survive the threats of the challenges they faced?
- What were those resources?
- Once the relationship succumbed to life stressors, did they have a way to resuscitate it either on their own or with the help of a support system?

At the beginning of the marriage, Muka had answered these questions in the affirmative, listing the many resources she believed they had at their disposal. However, the current state of their relationship had led her to realize she had been mistaken. From the very beginning, they had only assumed they had the resources they needed, and they hadn't been equipped to face a worse-case scenario.

I wanted to further explore the cultural and spiritual context of their relationship. They had shared a faith community, enjoyed the support of their families, and had a wide social network. Most importantly, they had loved each other. They had been equipped with scriptural principles and beliefs about marriage. In addition, they had taken relevant courses at the undergraduate and graduate level in the areas of behavioural sciences,

CHAPTER ELEVEN: MY ANALYSIS

human relationships, pastoral counselling, effective communication, and problem-solving skills. And somehow this had not been enough. In the end, their defences were depleted.

All of these misplaced assumptions were based on their shared values and approach to marriage and family relationships. In my assessment, I observed that the couple had been rooted in a self-healing cultural system, a system that was expected to survive without the need for professional healers, either traditional or contemporary. Such a system was expected to anticipate and address problems before they arose through the use of preventive therapeutic methods, and members of the extended network of family and friends were to be given the responsibility to help the couple address interpersonal conflicts.

In addition to being rooted in a cultural heritage with zero tolerance for separation and divorce, Muka and Akawd had been immersed in a faith tradition that discouraged infidelity and commended life-enhancing and supportive family relationships. Their culture stipulated many methods for maintaining healthy relationships. The application of love and respect was a key component in this strategy.

Culturally speaking, their marriage practices were different from those seen in modern western contexts. Mothers would walk their daughters to their weddings, helping their daughters to understand what they were getting into and providing counsel and guidance. Muka's mother had walked her to her humble wedding and continued to offer counsel and support throughout the marriage when opportunities presented themselves. Muka's mother-in-law had also supported the marriage and stood by her side in times of conflict.

Both Muka and Akawd maintained cordial relationships with their in-laws and were respected as leaders in their spiritual and social communities. Moreover, their spiritual beliefs and faith practices provided healthy guidance. They were both professing Christians by the time they met and had come into the relationship with a strong grounding in faith. It was assumed that they were starting their life together on a shared foundation. Their first line of defence in the face of expected life stressors would be the Scriptures, with their knowledge in behavioural sciences serving as a backup. Scripture stipulates how a person is to relate to and treat their parents, spouses, children, and communities as a whole. They resolved to treat each other the way they themselves would wish to be treated. They expected that selfless love and submission to one another would yield a healthy and stable environment, which would in turn ensure positive growth and development for all members of the family.

Not only were Akawd and Muka adherents in their faith communities, they were leaders. It was expected that they would lead by example. They held a place of esteem in their communities and were often approached by others for help and support.

As such, the assumptions they made at the beginning of their relationship seemed to have been understandable.

This kind of grounding didn't presuppose the absence of challenges or life stressors, of course. Rather, this approach was meant to anticipate challenges and give them effective tools to cope with them.

As a result of all this, Muka and Akawd had believed their marriage to be divorce-proof. No offence would have been considered severe enough to end the marriage. Brimming with love and forgiveness, it seemed to them that only one of their deaths could end it. Even in death, their relationship would continue, since their beliefs promised a reunion after death in a different state.

That's what they believed—until the unthinkable happened. The marriage suffered a devastating blow that destabilized every support system they had in place.

It was clear to me that Muka was still having a hard time determining which incident, if any, had delivered the final blow. Even in her grief, and with this very grim prognosis, she still seemed to be hoping for the best. In her own words, she had described herself as "still married, to a prodigal husband." Was she in denial?

As time went on, and I spoke further with Muka, I learned that Akawd seemed unable to produce some of the final documents required to finalize the divorce. In the meantime, he was now indicating a willingness to incorporate the wisdom of traditional elders in their lives.

Muka didn't know what to make of all this.

The judge had recently directed them to take the time needed to address the legal questions surrounding their shared property outside of Canada. That decision seemed to put the divorce on hold.

Was the marriage truly dead? To use medical terminology, it seemed there was at least some minimal brain activity in this dying patient, and maybe even an irregular but notable heartbeat. I had to agree with the analogy Muka had used—her marriage was in a coma.

But it had not yet been pronounced dead.

──── CONCLUSION ────

This analysis began on a grimmer note than it seems to be ending. While taking a close look at the marriage, I saw that it had taken ill when the spiritual, cultural, and legal aspects of the relationship came to be at odds with each other, the spiritual and cultural aligning themselves against the legal.

When Akawd first filed for divorce, Muka managed to delay the process on spiritual grounds. Even his family appealed his decision, based on their cultural practices. However, Akawd didn't seem to give any consideration to these arguments. He manipulated the legal system to allow him to drop his responsibilities as a husband and father, so that he could walk away without a sense of guilt or shame. He didn't attempt to engage in any of the prescribed approaches toward resolving the disagreements, nor did he establish the accuracy of his allegations. Similarly, his and Muka's cultural practices recommended exhausting family and extended family support systems to address their challenges, but he declined every proposal by Muka to explore the resources available to them. He opted for the legal path which seemed capable of granting him everything he wished for without requiring accountability.

Muka questioned the soundness of his judgments and decisions and wondered whether some other undetected physiological, psychological, or spiritual factors were impairing his ability to perceive the issues clearly. When she made this appeal, a lawyer dismissed it, saying, "Divorce is a right and anyone who asks for one is entitled to receive it, be they well or unwell." Similarly, a representative from the bankruptcy firm affirmed that her and Akawd's cultural practices had no place in the separation process or division of property.

It seemed clear to me that Muka had exhausted all avenues in attempting to delay the inevitable. Her rationale had been to give Akawd more time to process whatever it was that seemed to be impairing his judgment. She also explained to me that she would have preferred to address their challenges through their shared faith community instead of the legal profession. However, that was not to be the case.

She felt that the spiritual and cultural stances backing her marriage maintained the upper hand against the legal stance, but this didn't bring her any feelings of relief. She had hoped that Akawd would respect their faith precepts and cultural values enough to take them into consideration when making such important decisions. For over three decades, they had leaned on each other and navigated life as a team. They had achieved every accomplishment of their lives together. They had raised a family together! His insistence on taking the legal route puzzled her. She didn't know if the decision was a deliberate act to ensure a quick and simple separation or a desperate and convenient choice motivated by greed. Whatever the case, it placed them both in an awkward position, navigating foreign and hostile territory.

Muka told me how difficult it was to sit across a table from Akawd in a legal proceeding and listen to a stranger weigh their words and evaluate their decisions. She opted to represent herself, trusting that her clean conscience against Akawd's allegations and the stability of her faith in God would sustain her and determine her destiny. Even though the situation was unfamiliar and they were moving away from their cultural context and family supports, she retained hope.

While contemplating his decision to leave Muka, Akawd had gradually reduced his involvement with their faith community. He

CONCLUSION

had stopped attending church and participating in the life of their faith community. At the time, Akawd excused his behaviour by citing personal reasons. He dismissed the suggestion of seeking the support and direction of the church on the basis of his apparent disconnection from that community. Muka respected his wish and obliged with all the requirements and orders given by the court.

As a respondent, she had to present all the documents that were requested of her. She educated herself on the proceedings so that she could proceed with prudence. She consulted legal professionals to obtain information that would protect her and her children against potential blunders.

Meanwhile, Akawd didn't submit the required documents to the court, even as the deadlines loomed. In a brief meeting with Muka, he disclosed that he had come to the realization that he had made a big mistake when he made the heinous allegations against her. He was now struggling with the implications of his behaviour. He confessed that he couldn't proceed with the divorce application but didn't know how to clean up the mess. He was careful not to ask for forgiveness, but admitted that he knew he had no right to even expect to be forgiven.

Instead of the grim prognosis that had earlier pointed toward death, there suddenly arose a tiny hope of resuscitation. Muka had a new set of questions to ponder. Would this marriage ever wake up from its coma? What would it take to achieve this? How much damage had been inflicted? Going forward, what would be the state of the relationship?

Muka felt like she was entering another limbo. She had already made peace with her evolving marital status. What would happen if her prodigal husband did indeed return home?

──── AFTERWORD ────

While Akawd and Muka's divorce proceedings were put on hold, several life events occurred that required them to come together in support of their children. In one meeting, Akawd described to Muka an interesting experience. He had stumbled upon a book in a box of his personal belongings one day. The book was a text on spiritual warfare, a resource he had used during his ministry training. He picked up the book and noted that it was one of the few possessions he still had from his ministry resources.

The sight of the book triggered a memory of the last ministry project he had been involved in before the ordeal with his marriage had begun to unfold. The project had involved preparing for and then teaching a course on spiritual warfare. Akawd couldn't recall what exactly had become of the lessons and resources he'd used for the course. Over a period of four years, many of his personal belongings had been misplaced.

What he did remember, however, was the process of teaching the course. He recalled that preparing and presenting the course had been intense and physically exhausting. Knowing the significance of spiritual warfare, he now wondered if in the intervening years he had experienced a spiritual retaliation from that event.

This seemed to confirm Muka's hypothesis that he had been suffering from a mental breakdown—or rather, as the case may be, a spiritual meltdown. Had Akawd become a casualty of spiritual warfare, a victim of the very battle he had declared against the enemy of his soul?

This revelation helped bring both Muka and Akawd some insight into this puzzling nightmare. The pieces were starting to come together. Throughout the ordeal, Akawd's wrath toward Muka hadn't made sense. Perhaps Akawd's previous behaviours had catalyzed a spiritual attack on him—and by extension on their marriage and family. The attack had been so severe that she could only attribute her resilience and survival to God's grace.

──── OTHER BOOKS BY THE AUTHOR ────

ISBN 0-9782569-0-5
Away From Home is a memoir documenting the experiences of a family in migration. The journey begins with a dream for post graduate education and a desire to experience the world beyond. This temporary educational expedition leads the family to a university in Potchefstroom, South Africa, where they endeavour to settle, establish new relations and contextualize family traditions and routines. They encounter a detour that brings them to Ontario in Canada and they settle in a small town in Southwestern Ontario. This book seeks to highlight some of the challenges they faced, common to many immigrants, while also acknowledging the unique resources and support system availed to them by virtue of their faith in God and commitment to His people and service.

ISBN 1-60703-614-2
I'm Forgiven is an inspirational book that evolved from a life experience. The author highlights some of the steps that may lead a Christian away from God, and opens up a discussion on biblical solutions, as the only way back into fellowship with God. The choice to get back on track

and proceed forward by maintaining a closer walk with God is highly recommended. The words that evolved into this book emerged from a combination of the lessons learnt by the author from a life experience and, relevant examples from the Bible coupled with some contemporary realities.

ISBN 978-1-926676-97-5

Beneath the Cracks is a biography highlighting situations in life that presented perfect recipes for failure. The author takes a look back at some of the episodes in her life that turned into, or opened up cracks wide enough to nip her in. Instead, the experience beneath the cracks provided a "time-out" that made room for deep reflections and translated deep thoughts into written words. While the experiences remained as daunting as it gets and sometimes the way out was never direct or obvious; the end has always brought renewed blessings, insight and commitment to her calling.

Death Did Us Part presents a short story about the tumultuous marital relationship of a couple at the brink of divorce. The book, based on a true story, is a reflection on some of the pitfalls that plagued the marriage of Akawd and Muka and brought it to its deathbed. Akawd and Muka were both committed Christians and leaders in their church when they immigrated to Canada from Africa.

By sharing this story, I provide an opportunity for readers to both understand better and observe the parallels that might exist between their own relationships and this couple's. My hope is that these patterns may then be named and externalized. The book also serves to celebrate marriages and the couples who keep their vows.

Rev. (Dr.) Florence A. Juma is a registered psychotherapist in Ontario, Canada. She is ordained with Pentecostal Assemblies of Canada (PAOC), serves as a certified spiritual care practitioner in the hospital, and an Associate Professional Faculty at Martin Luther University College.

ISBN 978-1-4866-1798-2